RAPE!

One Victim's Story

RAPE!

One Victim's Story

A DOCUMENTARY
by W. Ware Lynch

FOLLETT PUBLISHING COMPANY
Chicago

Manufactured in the United States of America.
Library of Congress Catalog Card Number: 74-78582
ISBN: 0-695-80491-X
First Printing

Dr. Robert Miller, Diplomate of the American Board of Neurology and Psychiatry, is a Fellow of the New York Academy of Medicine and a Fellow of the American Psychiatric Association.

For the past ten years, he has worked with the Connecticut Department of Mental Health and for the past five years, has been Superintendent of Fairfield Hills Hospital. During this time, in addition to being on the faculty at Yale University College of Medicine, he has also taught at the State Police Training Academy, has been on the liaison committee between the Bar Association and the State Medical Society, and has testified in more than 1,000 felony cases in both state and federal courts.

In addition he is frequently consulted by municipal, state, and federal enforcement agencies seeking assistance in constructing psychiatric profiles which might assist in the apprehension of unknown perpetrators.

In Connecticut, the statutes on rape have been changed to remove the need for corroboration. Until this change, in the words of Chief State's Attorney Joseph Gormley, a man who broke into an apartment, assaulted a lone female occupant, raped her, and left after stealing her TV set, could be charged with and convicted of breaking and entering, assault and robbery, but not rape, unless corroboration was available.

In Bangladesh, thousands of Pakistani women, raped during the last war in that area, are condemned to prostitution or starvation, since they are considered unmarriageable or, had they been married, no longer acceptable though they were helpless victims.

In fact, with the exception of one tribe in the South Pacific noted by anthropologists for utilizing rape as a substitute for courtship, no society accepts rape as a reasonable act.

Whereas in times of war, rape may be condoned by pseudo-civilized armies, even there the majority of civilized people not only helps the victims but also punishes the perpetrators.

If one can be detached about such an emotion-laden subject, rape is a curious paradox in that it is a sex crime in which the sex act is predicated on motivation which only remotely could be considered sexual.

Rape is an act predicated on fear, hatred, and revenge. Whatever pleasures are derived stem from the vanquishing, hurting, and debasement of the victim as a "proof" that the perpetrator is more powerful than his victim, and revenge in that he is capable of humiliating and forcing victims to submit against their will. This is of course in contradiction to his having believed as a young man that women were powerful and dominant, making him feel resentfully helpless.

The essential paradox here is that aggressive, assaultive acts stem from a reaction to passive, submissive character development. A man does not commit rape unless he fears and hates women.

Further, as normal sex has fewer taboos attached to it today, more and more rapists force victims into more diversified sexual acts, such as sodomy, which are considered shameful or debasing to and by the victim.

In almost thirty years of psychiatric practice in both office and institution, I have psychiatrically examined countless rape victims and rapists. Almost invariably the lives of the victims were disrupted and a profound emotional disturbance was produced. But on the other hand, very few rapists could not be legally considered insane, as most states define the requirements for finding someone not guilty by reason of insanity. Most rapists I have examined are not "lacking in substantial capacity by reason of mental disease or disorder to know the wrongfulness of their acts or to conform them to the requirements of the law." These stipulations, by the way, are the requirements in most states for finding someone not guilty by reason of insanity.

Since most rapists are "characterologically" disturbed, it is my profound belief that alterations in their behavior can be effected most successfully by forcing them to learn that they have to accept responsibility for their acts and that unpleasant consequences will ensue from antisocial behavior.

Hopefully, the revisions in laws related to rape will enable more successful prosecutions, and these will not only act as a deterrent and remove dangerous persons from society, but also assist convicted rapists in refraining from repeated acts when they are released.

DR. ROBERT MILLER
Superintendent
Fairfield Hills Hospital
Newtown, Connecticut
May 28, 1974

I want to especially acknowledge the cooperation of Peter Marc Stern for his technical assistance in the preparation of this book.

W. W. L.

Attorney Peter Marc Stern lives in Manhattan. Mr. Stern is a graduate of Wharton School of Finance and Commerce in Philadelphia, Pa., and graduated cum laude from Syracuse College of Law, where he was the editor of the Syracuse Law Journal. *He practices in New York's courts, concentrating on criminal and bankruptcy cases.*

As a practicing attorney specializing in criminal law, I have seen the story in this book occur and reoccur with ever-increasing frequency. Rape is the fastest growing crime in the United States, and probably one with the lowest conviction ratio. Feminists have pointed to the antiquity and prejudicial nature of the laws relating to rape, and no doubt these laws have contributed to some extent to the present situation.

But now the laws are changing with great rapidity. In the large majority of states, corroboration of the rape, the penetration, the use of force, and the identification of the perpetrator by independent witnesses or circumstances is no longer required. The inherent bias of the common law to disbelieve the female, simply because it was thought that she would use the rape laws to ensnare the male, is being discarded. We now say that the female is as worthy of belief as any complainant in any other type of case.

Other suggestions as to modification of the law are also appearing daily from all quarters. It has been suggested that rape cases be heard by a panel of judges, rather than by a jury. It has been suggested that no spectators be permitted in the courtroom. It has been suggested that the defendant and the alleged victim no longer confront each other face to face in the courtroom, although cross-examination would be conducted by the defendant's attorney. And in New York, one legislator has suggested that if it can be shown that the defendant had a prior relationship of any kind with the complainant, that corroboration of all elements still be required. Some of these proposed changes are of such a nature that they would require amendment of both the United States Constitution as well as state constitutions. All of them arise from good motives.

I personally would recommend the establishment of

a Rape Victim's Indemnification Corporation to be set up by the respective states. The conviction of a rapist will rarely help to heal the wounds which his victim has endured. And the convictions are so rare as to afford these victims hardly any solace at all. A common law civil action for assault usually results in an uncollectible judgment. The rapist has no assets to collect. While an award of money damages would certainly not erase the horror and embarrassment of the incident from the victim's mind, it would at least accomplish something better than what we have at the present time, which is nothing. The system of compensation would provide money damages for pain, suffering, and mental distress to victims of forcible rapes, whether or not the defendant was identified, apprehended, or convicted, the sole criteria being whether a forcible rape was committed upon the claimant. We are tempted to say that such a law would yield many fraudulent claims, but such is the risk of any social legislation of this type, and it is far better to compensate the vast majority of legitimate claims rather than to penalize all rape victims. If, of course, a perpetrator had assets, he would reimburse the corporation, if convicted.

Lastly, this writer and the readers of this book must concern themselves with what can be done in the area of the law to remedy the present situation. Unfortunately, it is the opinion of this writer that the law can do very little; that the job is up to society as a whole, a combination of social attitudes and prejudices which combine to place the victim rather than the defendant on trial. The jury will usually look to the background and character of the victim rather than the accused, and unless the defendant elects to testify, nothing can be revealed about his background. Even if he elects to testify, the only elements of his background which can be brought before the jury are prior convictions. But juries, particularly women, suspect the victim of having invited and even enjoyed the act. Anything particularly sexual, a hint of immorality, or even a seductive appearance relieves the defendant. The juries apply a standard of absolute purity and chastity which they would not apply to themselves.

The greatest protection which our system of criminal law has to offer is the trial jury. Juries are neither stupid nor naive; they are *you*, sensitive and intelligent people. Only by elimination of innate prejudices and biased social attitudes can any progress be made towards putting rapists where they belong. The dropping of the requirement of corroboration helps somewhat, but the basic answer lies in society.

The story in this book has happened a thousand times, and it will happen a thousand times more, but it is not the fault of the law that it happens, or is permitted to happen. Understaffed prosecutors' offices must be supplied with a greater number of more experienced attorneys, and their salaries must be commensurate with their tasks. Well-paid defense attorneys will fight hard for their clients; they are being paid to do so. They will dedicate long hours of research and attention to their cases, and the least that the People can do is to place their prosecutors in a position to do likewise.

Rape is not a dirty joke; it is a brutal assault of the highest magnitude upon the privacy of a woman. Enforcement officers, prosecutors, and society must take it more seriously.

PETER MARC STERN
New York, New York
May 28, 1974

The story of Susan Landress is a compilation of facts and decisions from the following cases: *People* v. *Yannuci*, *People* v. *Dohring*, *People* v. *Masse*, *People* v. *Deitch*, *People* v. *Powell* ("Criminal Law in the State of New York"). These facts involved the defense attorney's argument and the subsequent judicial findings.

One

It was "wrap-up" time and she had twenty seconds.

She watched the sweep hand race to the close of her segment and knew her producer would be calling for a tight close-up, for it was Monday. Today, as every Monday, she would finish her broadcast with an announcement of her series subject for the weeks to come.

The screen displayed a petite woman in her late twenties; brown closely cropped hair swept upwards away from well-formed cheekbones, a long neck. Her deep amber eyes focused directly at the camera— excited, determined, honest. Traditionally, her lips were pursed. Her viewers knew the expression. It was one of a woman with a long interest span when once set on a path. She had done in-depth features on women and drugs, alcoholism in the suburbs, divorce, and other female traumas. Her determination to report the truth and her sometimes shocking frankness had elevated her from a commonplace news reporter to the leading exponent of "the woman's angle" on nationwide TV.

In Patricia's mind, millions of women were leaning a little bit closer to their television sets and men in the room had been shushed, for the mail told her that her subjects had hit home.

The finger sliced down, the camera light came on, and Patricia began:

"This coming week we are going to explore one of the most explosive issues facing women today. I urge you to join me when we examine a problem that becomes terror for some woman every fifteen minutes in the United States. I'm talking about rape! Please join me next Monday. Until then, this is Patricia Rankin for Group One News. Good evening."

On the balcony of Le Cafe des Artistes, where murals by the late Howard Chandler Christie lent an air of frivolity to the serious business which was conducted beneath them, Patricia soon sat with her producer, Joseph Serpe Fontana. He had accepted her weekly series under mild protest. "Even though the subject is getting more and more attention, I think rape is a fad. It'll pass."

"Like murder?" she asked, sweetly. "Or maybe kidnapping?"

Joe had already told his boss he always gave Rankin a free hand. "She knows women. We don't. Look at her ratings."

"It's a major Women's Liberation thing. The laws are the crux," she added to soothe him. Then she reminded, "Male attitudes are basic, should be explored. Sometimes I don't think we've progressed socially since the first caveman grabbed his first sex-object by the hair and took what he wanted."

Joe sat toying with his glass of Poulle Fume, thinking how affirmative she was, yet how feminine.

4

He was coming along, caught up in her enthusiasm, and she knew it. She tucked a hair into place, ready to continue, but waited her turn.

"Patricia, do you mean rape is as gross, as violent as a beast reacting to a primitive animal reflex?"

"Sorry about that last word. What happens isn't a reflex. If that were so you couldn't blame the man, but only the circumstances surrounding the confrontation. No, Joe, the shrinks call it 'a trigger' which activates something which is present all the time. The rapist finds the first available woman. If the girl walking down the street happens to be you, you're it!"

She noticed how deeply interested Joe Fontana had become. It was a reaction Patricia was getting used to, for she knew that forcible rape was interesting, disturbing, and had power over the imagination. The subject had been so delicately handled by the press that most people really knew very little about it.

"Women have a different view about rape than men, Joe," she said. "We are accused of creating the occasion of our victimization. Our society views rape in the fantasy category rather than in the social context. What I intend to cover, along with a thorough study of the inadequate laws, is the relationship between the rapist and his available female victim."

"I thought men always raped . . . utter strangers. I mean they see an attractive girl. . . ."

"Joe, that's part of the male fantasy, a kind of blue movie men lock into their heads. The relationship is important. And I'll get into that in the section we have called 'Victim-Rapist Relationship' coming up in part five.

"But the main thing about this series is that I'm not just going to expose the problem. Women know about the problem. What I have to tell them is what to do about it. How to avoid the situation, how to defend

5

themselves, what to do if they are raped, how to handle themselves in court. Just understanding it isn't going to solve this problem. . . ."

Patricia leaned forward earnestly, the sweetness drawn from her face. Her voice rose, and her eyes flashed. A passerby would have thought her to be an angry wife berating her husband. But Joe Fontana knew the look and recognized the manner. When Patricia got involved with her subjects, she became totally involved, and this enthusiasm, this caring attitude, was what had boosted her ratings, and those of the whole news show.

"Joe, you probably think like a lot of men think, and I'm warning you, when Patricia Rankin starts on rape, she's going to debunk the fantasies and hit hard. The poor victim today has no chance. No woman can walk the streets or accept a male relationship without living defensively. God knows the law and men force her into this.

"Right now, Joe, some girl is being attacked in a New York street because she got in the way of a man more murderous, in my mind, than a mob 'hit' man. And when he's through with her, and when the police and the hospitals and the courts are through with her, she'll have been subjected to more disgrace and humiliation and torture than any woman since the Salem Witch Hunts or the Spanish Inquisition. And it's going on, right now, out there!"

Joe shrugged, and downed his wine. This was going to be rough on him and the rest of the male staff, but terrific for the ratings.

Susan Landress had been doing a lot of thinking during the last hour. Locked inside an inverted shoe box of a room in the singles country in Manhattan,

6

bordered by York and First, she was stifled, up-tight, anxious to communicate, to join activities visible all around her. Her roommate, who in fact she hardly knew yet, was gone, a stewardess off around the world. Susan envied her freedom and her sophistication, and wished she could be anywhere, anywhere else but cramped up in this stuffy little apartment.

On the street other young people were laughing, gathering outside Friday's and Adam's Apple. They met, dated, and walked away arm in arm. She envied them all. This was their city, not hers. They were free here; she was trapped. Out in Santa Monica, her city, her life had begun falling apart at a time when a woman could expect to "get it all together."

But all that was long ago. Now she was here in New York, whether she liked it or not, feeling very much like a statistic on inflow of population to the urban centers.

She saw herself as she had been, long-legged, sun-bleached hair falling to her shoulders, dressed in her perpetual jeans or bikini, striding happily down the night beach at Malibu, passing the couples on the rocks, seeking her own consolation in exercise to loosen any mental block. There, in the dark, she would pass the well-lit chalets which lined the exclusive shore, hear a dog bark, a car speed along the Pacific Coast Highway, maybe a siren after it, the surf curling white and languid and sweeping silently up to touch her flying feet. Back home was her mother, an invalid since the car accident which brought in some insurance money. Somewhere on the Santa Monica Pier fishing, or in a bar talking about fishing, was her father, bent with the ravages of early arthritis, living on welfare, and selling his stories for another beer. Overseas, her brother-hero

Dougie—Douglas Ghent, sergeant in the Air Force, two citations—coming home to a job pumping gas!

And when he came home, he had put everything he had ever done or earned on the line for her—"My sweet, attractive, but stupid little Sue."

She couldn't stay cooped up any longer. She decided to go for a walk, to think things out. She slipped into shorts, a blouse, a pair of sandals, and grabbed a cotton blazer.

Maybe it wouldn't be so bad. She could "explore" the city like a new section of cliff, a sand dune, or beach. Out on the Coast she had done this a lot, biking out to Malibu, walking through underbrush, over fences to the surf, discovering new places to ride the waves.

Susan took a deep breath of the heavy city air and bravely set out in the direction of the East River. Down there she sensed the familiarity of water. A tug honked once and warned a passing freighter it would pass to portside. There was a responding whistle from a freighter. Behind her she left the delighted screams of a young woman laughing at a boy's joke. Behind lay the lights of the singles cafes; ahead, darkness.

Susan finally went on into the park, down a semicircular path where a small light flickered under the leaves of a tree. As in Santa Monica, she'd think things out. Soon all the hangups would be gone, she'd get a job, meet a nice guy. She wouldn't always be a stranger in the city.

Suddenly there was an onrushing of air, the noise of pounding feet. A weight was thrown against her legs from behind. A strong arm locked around her throat and Susan was thrown with violence to the ground. A man's heavy body fell on top of her. She tried to scream.

8

"Right here under the what to dos and what nots
..." Patricia was saying, laying down a last page of
the script due to be heard five weeks hence, "it says
to plan and execute your protection. 'You have thirty
seconds. That's all. If he grabs for your throat, for
example, and he's facing you, don't reach for his
wrists. It's instinctive but don't do it! Thrust upwards
at his Adam's apple or at the underside of his nose
with the heel of your hand. Or go for his eyes with
your nails. With violence! Quickly. Spit in his eyes.
He will invariably stop long enough to wipe it off.
This is your chance! Run!'"

Susan's breath was cut off almost completely. Suddenly, she felt as if she was going to die. Yet she
couldn't scream because the man's arm cut off her
windpipe. She couldn't use her arms to defend herself
from the sudden attack because one arm was locked
beneath her own body and his left hand held her right
wrist in a viselike grip. Unable to breathe properly,
unable to move, she panicked. Her mind refused to
accept what was happening. She felt hands at her
blouse, heard the man's grunt, knew her shorts were
being pulled from her. His teeth bit into her. She tried
to scream. The pain was unbearable. He plunged into
her, brutally, abrasively. She gathered enough
strength to cry out. But she made no sound.
She was unconscious of anything except pain and
frustration at her inability to stop the continuing
attack. He threw her face down and fell upon her
back while she lay half-conscious. Susan knew she
was bleeding; she tasted the blood, felt hard stones
against her body. Now she was free to cry out. Then
he attacked her again. My God, this wasn't happening! He thrust fiercely into her. She blanked out.

Later she heard footsteps running away, the whistle of a tugboat. Then utter silence. A moment later she became conscious of being hurt in many parts of her body and then of someone screaming, wailing. She rolled on her back and sobbed.Then she heard approaching footsteps. He was coming back!

"Good God!" said a woman's voice over her in the dark. Then Susan felt a Kleenex wiping her mouth, another at her eyes, and the woman said, "You poor thing. Let me help you. Here, turn this way."

She was lifted to her feet. The woman, slim and dark, seemed very efficient and kind. She said she was a nurse. "Do as I say now, dear. Come along. Put on these things." Susan pulled on her shorts with great effort, found her sandals and blouse. "Is this yours?" It was her blazer.

Thirty minutes later Susan lay on a soft bed in the woman's deluxe high-rise apartment. She had been led gingerly past the doorman, up the high-speed shaft to the quarters of Julia McElroy, a tall, middle-aged woman who had taken charge of the situation.

"We have to get you to a hospital right away. You have to be examined, then report the crime to the police."

Susan only knew one thing. She didn't want anyone to touch her—most certainly not a man. And the idea of having been involved in a crime of any sort, even as a victim, just didn't make sense.

She sat up in bed. "Police? Not me. I'm going home."

But Julia was already using the yellow princess telephone, dialing the numbers defiantly, angrily. That bastard was not going to get away with this if she had anything to do with it. The poor girl. She turned to Susan and held the phone away from her mouth.

10

"Now you be quiet and leave things to me. You need to be tested for sperm sample specimens, and treated for bruises and the doctor will testify—at the trial."

"What trial?"

Julia was talking. "I want to report a rape."

What was happening? Susan wanted out. She started to get up. Julia stood over her, efficient and commanding. She was strong and motherly, and though Susan wanted to leave, she knew she was in good hands.

"Stay there. I've notified the police. Hospital next. There's one right across the street. The police know about it now. After the examination, you'll go to the precinct house and they'll take a report from you. Sergeant Mulcahy. Come with me."

"Okay," Susan sighed, and reluctantly followed the woman out the door.

Ten minutes later they were in the hospital. The nurse made her wait on a bench while Julia filled in a sheet and kept asking for a doctor to examine her. "It's rape," she said in hushed tones, as if Susan had been discovered to be a carrier of jungle rot or typhoid.

Then they sat her down in a wheelchair and pushed her through the hallways, with Julia chattering away, until they reached the examination room. She waited twenty minutes. "You're not the only one," Julia said, but it didn't make Susan feel any better.

The doctor was hasty. He looked her over while she lay on the examination table; her feet in the stirrups, and Susan kept wondering why the other men weren't sent away. Julia took her to a wall and held her hand while another man reeled off what he saw on her half-exposed body as to "bruises and abrasions," describing their color, size, and location to the first doctor who wrote the observations down, scribbling with a pencil. Why did she have to go through all this, and why weren't they out looking for the man?

"We got a good specimen." The doctor handed a slide to the nurse. "Be certain you don't get the names mixed up. This is Susan Landers."

"L-A-N-D-R-E-S-S," spelled Julia. "Her last name is 'Landress'." The doctor smiled. "Thank you, miss. We'll remember it." Then he said to his nurse, "Who's next?"

They helped Susan out. No wheelchair. Just a strong black attendant and Julia. At the door Julia urged her to spend the rest of the night with her. "Right after the police thing."

"I want to go home," is all she said, hoping she didn't sound ungrateful. But she'd had enough of strangers messing with her life.

At the precinct house, Susan felt like she was entering the set of a B motion picture. Men were all over the place, in blue trousers, black shoes, and blue shirts, looking young and wearing guns under their arms, radios on their belts. They raced about, letting her pass politely; some of them with more than a passing look. Susan was used to it now. Julia took her to the man at the desk called "stationhouse superintendant."

Later in the squad room upstairs she gave the three men a complete description. They seemed mildly interested.

"He wore a black button-down sweater and a sweaty t-shirt. I couldn't see his face too well. But I did see that he had thick eyebrows that met in the middle of his nose. He had black curly hair and a squarish jaw and face. Of course it was dark, like you say. Yes, I know it is difficult to give 'positive identification.' Maybe it is. I don't know. But he squinted when he looked at me as he . . . turned me over and he definitely was tall. I'd say six feet, anyway."

One man took down everything she said, then flipped the cover closed on his memo pad and said, "Okay, lady. Thanks."

Julia took her home. She waited while Susan undressed again and took a shower. Julia opened her bed. Clean and aching, Susan made it to the bed and literally fell in it.

"I'll call you from time to time," Julia said. "I'll be around, if you need me. This city is a real hassle. You gotta be careful, honey. You better get up and lock the door after me." For a minute she stood in the open doorway, her trim silhouette framed in the light, then she closed the door. Susan obediently followed orders, double-locked the door, and returned to bed. What more could possibly happen to me, she wondered, and turned toward the wall to cry.

On her way back to her apartment, Julia knew she would have to get out of New York. A lot of her friends in Germany and Switzerland reading stories about street crime in the city had pleaded with her to leave, "before you're murdered in cold blood!"

She knew she really didn't belong here; she had actually never become a part of the city's tough fabric. She had never come to terms with the ever-present violence of Manhattan. Maybe she wasn't tough enough, or didn't want to become tough enough to make it here. It could have been me, she thought, as she rode the elevator in her maximum-security high rise. It really could have been me out there in the park. She called her sister in Connecticut as soon as she was home, to make sure her two children visiting there for the week were safe and happy, and then set about making plans to leave the city for good.

13

The long distance operator reported Dr. Fullerton was in residence in Gstaadt and would be there for her call in ten minutes.

"Hello, Bud," she said when he answered. "I'm going to accept your invitation. I'll be leaving soon. I'll let you know when I'll be there."

When she hung up her face was flushed and her heart beat with excitement. She might as well face it. He offered security. Besides, he loved her children almost as much as he loved her. Julia went into her bathroom, took a long, hot shower, tried to concentrate on her new life, but couldn't get her mind off Susan. She would be saved from a future in this horrible city, but what about that poor girl? Julia knew that brutal episode would never end for Susan. Those ten minutes of terror would color the rest of her life.

Susan's mind reeled back, away from New York, back to Santa Monica. She never should have come here. Santa Monica had been home to her since she was born. She never thought about leaving, but maybe she knew she would.

Her mother, from her bed, had often nagged her about earning money even when she was little. She recalled one conversation which had started out with her mother telling her there was a new candy store opening at the corner. "It's named Gigi's Specials. Why don't you ask if you can work there?" The conversation had ended in tears on both sides.

"I know, Mom, but I can't. It's against the law for me to work, and what can I learn in a stupid candy store?"

"I know they passed a law that your father couldn't lift a finger to help us, but I didn't know. . . ."

14

Dougie had interrupted. "I've saved enough from my Air Force pay so she can continue school 'til she graduates. And leave Pops out of this."

Yes, Dougie had always defended his father. Maybe as a man he knew what it must be like to come home to a complaining invalid. She had watched her older brother get up at six, make his bed, and go off to pump gas at the Sunset and Pacific Coast Highway Texaco station, then serve food at The Chart House until one. "Enjoy yourself now, kid," he'd say. "It's all downhill after high school."

Each day after school, Susan and her gang had grown up on the beach and in the surf, their brown, healthy bodies melting into the tan and the blonde hair of hundreds of others, surfboards tipped precariously from the rear end of VWs, laughter preceding and following them; they had been carefree. Then Bradley Landress had come into her life and Susan Ghent began to think of herself as "Susan Landress."

"Your Flemish ancestors would turn in their ancient graves," her mother had warned. "I know he's 'beautiful' and has a TR4, whatever that is. I hope it's decent; but God knows where he comes from!"

But Bradley had determination and he soon traded in his TR4 for a Ford truck. Then after working in the Malibu Hills Farms long enough to acquire a bank account, after three long absences during winters, he had "come out of the hills to get his bride," as he had said it.

Half asleep, Susan gritted her teeth.

The wedding. Mother in a wheelchair, Dougie with his uniform and all those ribbons, even Pop in a blue suit, holding her by the arm down the aisle, and Pastor Ginzell intoning, "Who giveth this woman?"

Not until halfway between Dallas and Fort Worth

15

did the dream vanish. "I hope you don't mind. Please don't be angry," her husband Brad had started, "but it'll be just you and me now, won't it, no matter what?"

Frozen for some reason, though it was eighty degrees out there, she had asked, "Why shouldn't it be?"

"Well, . . . that is, she wouldn't let me get a divorce . . . so."

It had come spilling out, and even though he had cried—Brad, big roughneck that he was, had cried—she couldn't get over it. Insanely and without thought, she had lept from the car at the nearest coffee shop while Brad went to the bathroom and had raced to the pay telephone booth.

When he came out, her farewell note was stuck in the windshield wiper.

In her pocket she had two hundred in cash, a wedding present from Dougie's pay. With that she had hired an Avis rent-a-car and driven until she was in Fort Worth. There Dougie's money order at Western Union got her the ticket to New York. It had been a kind of race. A race to reach "the spires and shimmering lights above New York."

"There you'll be happy and get away from us all. We're provincial here and you've learned your lesson. It's been hard. Don't believe anyone any more. Except me!" Dougie had warned her. Now look at her. How could she face him, or Mom, or even Pops for that matter? In twenty-one years she had managed to completely ruin her life, and she couldn't imagine how it could possibly get any worse. Finally, she fell asleep.

Two

The driver was black, Police Officer Paul Bernard, graduate of the Academy ten years ago, big hands gripping the wheel, his teeth set, and his jaw muscles bulging, tense because they were about to make another collar. In his left-hand breast pocket was a picture of his mother, a comb which he used often in his short cropped hair, and an emergency dime for a pay phone. In his left was a mirror.

His partner, Pete Melo, was from a grocery family in the Bronx, wholesale. He was the only "cop" in his large family, though fifty percent of the men in his precinct house and at the Academy were Italians who had chosen law and order because of the steady pay and to counter slurs against the Mafia. In Pete's case, he wanted "bread."

On the dashboard facing the blue-eyed descendant of a proud family from Firenze was a series of photos of cop-killers. It was there to remind them . . . and for immediate identification.

In the back seat of the blue car with bubbles turning and sirens at a wail sat a dark-haired man they had picked up on a "probable cause"; namely, "attempted burglary and trespass." They'd rush the bastard to the station house, then cover their sector until 4:00 A.M., a gloomy prospect but routine.

They had responded to a call from Central, apprehended their suspect without resistance, spread his legs with a night stick, made him lean against the wall just outside Adam's Apple with all the singles jeering and yapping at their heels, and now they were on their way to the Seventeenth, their precinct house.

He had been read his rights. Now he would be booked. They would check the sheets for record of arrests and convictions, then tomorrow he would be arraigned.

"Out, you slob!" bellowed Melo, and dealt a blow to the suspect's back which sent him spinning across the sidewalk and into the station. There they stood before the desk attendant.

Barnum saw that they had really caught a big fish. He was over six feet, heavily built, maybe two hundred pounds, and mean looking; his thick black brows met over his nose, and under their heavy curve squinted dull black eyes. As he stood there, shifting from foot to foot, exuding a kind of alcoholic perspiration, he sniffled and wiped at his nose with thick fingers.

It was clear to Bernard that he could have put up quite a resistance, but for some reason, was near unconsciousness. Sometimes when guys were apprehended, he remembered, they got nauseous and came on like sissies.

"Name?" the desk attendant asked.

"Guy Masters."

"Spell it."

"G-U-Y. M-A-. . . ."

"All right!" Murphy was doing duty at the desk. He began writing. He hated the work.

"Address?"

Masters didn't answer. Bernard watched him slowly slouch forward and grabbed him. Melo gave Masters a small rabbit punch in the kidney and he pulled up.

"You asking for medical care?"

"What?" Masters had a streak of dried blood running from under his nose.

"Where do you live, Masters?"

"113635 Main, Bridgeport, Connecticut."

"Book him!" interrupted Melo. "Put it down; it came over Central. A citizen named Ray Murray is coming down to give an ID. Says it was an attempted trespass and a burglary."

"I was trying to take a leak, jeeeze. . ."

It was the first understandable sentence he had uttered. The men stopped talking and looked him over again. The action interested three men going off duty. One of them came over. It was Joe Gerlach.

"Is this the rape suspect?" Gerlach had a memory like an elephant.

"What rape?" droned Murph from the desk. He didn't want complications.

"Rape One. An APB. Just now. A girl was raped in the park near York and Sixty-second. This guy fits the description."

The sergeant came over. This was something for him. "Book him on the original suspicion. We'll hold him overnight for questioning. Remember, 'with no reasonable delay'." The men laughed. Gerlach stood there while Murph, an older hand and one who never wanted to do paper work, wrote things down very carefully. Melo, taller than Masters, kept looking over his head at his partner and smiling. Rapes were common. But they wouldn't be out in the car now for the rest of the night. It would be a change.

The sergeant came back with the rape complaint papers. You couldn't hit or threaten a guy charged with a crime and you couldn't place him under a hot light or in an uncomfortable or compromising position or browbeat him. But a rapist was at the bottom of the ladder with his men, and he knew what was about to happen. They'd need his confession.

"I want to make a telephone call," Masters demanded.

"What telephone call?" Murphy had known a rapist once. The guy was really a grind in school, a kind of queer. He had molested a young girl, dragged her into the boys' washroom. Later, the fellows in school had beat him up. Rapists were guys who freaked out on women, couldn't handle the idea of sex with them like a real man should; so they took it out on helpless girls or kids.

Masters still insisted on his call. "I seen it on TV. A guy gets the right to make one call."

Murph pointed to the pay telephone on the wall. The men found seats on the bench. Masters put in a dime. He dialed "O."

"Hey, you!" snapped Murph from his perch. "What you dialing the operator for? This ain't no game." Rapists caused more trouble than killers. A rapist was a real fuck-up, a mixed-up guy with "a terrific sex drive." In a strange way, Murph envied him.

"I need a number!" Masters was getting sober and now a little tired of being yelled at and cuffed around.

20

A big man, he would soon assert himself. "And I get one call."

"He gets three," said Bernard, who had been studying law. The rapist was a man who needed psychiatric care. If this guy was ever convicted and they sent him for psychological examination, they would find this out. Chances are, he would go free like they all did.

Besides, thought Bernard, they should let him have all his rights. No assistant DA would investigate the pre- or post-arrest factors, but his defense attorney would, even if he accepted Legal Aid. Those guys were sharper than most criminal lawyers as to rights.

"I want a Mrs. Raleigh McMurtry," Masters was saying to the long distance operator. "She lives in Greenwood Park in Boston Plains, near Boston, Mass. Tell her it's her son calling."

Three times he tried, and each time the line was busy.

"Get him some water," one of them said, because Masters was getting dizzy and was leaning against the wall. "No," said Murph, "take him upstairs to the interrogation room. He has to be questioned."

Upstairs they sat him on a chair like he had had in school with the right arm forming a small desk. He smiled at them, but the men crowding in the room weren't looking. One took off his coat. Masters saw the big revolver, a .38, under his arm.

Someone came in with water and handed it to the suspect.

"Christ!" Masters exploded and spit it out. "It's boilin' hot." He dropped the paper cup.

Masters stood up and brushed specks of water from his black cardigan sweater. Then a cop came up behind him and gave him a sharp knuckle blow to the left kidney.

Masters swung. Three men grabbed him and held him. They pushed him into the chair and he quieted down.

The man on his right pulled Masters's arm away from the chair and twisted it. There was a snap, and Masters doubled over in pain.

The man who did it, Steve Allbright, was an English major and had studied psychology. He knew that a rapist, to *medical science*, was one of society's misfits. He was what the book had called "a sadist" or "a man who bears tremendous hostility to women and needs to prove his mastery over them." Well no damned rapist would "prove his mastery" in Allbright's precinct and get away with it. Let him go lurk in corners at the Playboy Club or get his jollies at a porn movie. But lay off the girls. Allbright grimaced as he thought of this guy being sadistic to that point and striking down a woman, maybe the kid next door.

"Go ahead and question the suspect," said the sergeant. He was all business. They had thirty-two minutes 'til roll call.

They lowered a swivel light over his head. It shone in the middle of Masters's skull, hot and near to his brain. Then suddenly they all got up and moved out, leaving him alone in that position. At the door, Allbright said, "Don't move."

Masters was left in the locked room like that for two hours. He took off his sweater and moved away from the light. He began to wonder if he'd ever reach his mother. Why was she always on the phone? Gab, gab, gab! But men liked her. Her last husband, even more than his father. She could twist them all around her little finger.

He took out a handkerchief and blew hard. He pushed it back in his pocket and wondered about the next few hours. Would they really put him in jail? Would it be like in the movies with bulls and queers? He made up his mind he'd never go—no, not ever! He shook his big head like a prize fighter after a heavy blow, wiped at his nostrils like boxers do to start the mucus, and sat down.

He remembered how scrawny he was as a kid. How he watched Joe Louis fight and beat the tar out of every white and black man without boasting, like the others did nowadays. He was Joe Louis, quiet, huge, and something to be contended with when aroused. He, Guy Masters, would go to sleep now even if they had tried to bait him like a lion—but unlike the lion, he would remain cool, faking his physical condition and his mental reaction to these ignorant slobs, but knowing just who he was and what he was—until Mom arrived. She had always been the Marines over the hill or Gangbusters at the last minute, pulling him out of that private school when they found the pinups and his camera. She hadn't cared what they said. He was her boy. And she was his mother.

Three men came back. One was a big cop named Cluett. Cops called him "Clue." He came over and shook Masters awake. "Up!" The room was hot and smelled of perspiration. He took off his coat, sat down, and threw a thick leg over the arm of the chair facing the accused.

"Stay there, punk. Now you're going to confess." Punks like this were easy. You remind them of the scene, how good it was to make it with a girl, and they got all hot inside, and smackeroo—out would come the confession, because rapists had to talk about it.

The girls they made were sex symbols, even if they were ugly. As a matter of fact, Cluett kind of liked to talk to a suspect about "the act." He hadn't had a good piece in a long while, himself.

"What did you say . . . sir?" asked Masters. He sat up.

"You got a big head, mister, if you think you can knock off a broad in this area and get away with it. Now just tell us. . .." Cluett motioned to one of the other men. It was Percival, Charles Percival, the guy who was studying to be a detective and wanted to "make the gold shield" in the worst way.

"Here, Perc, take down his confession." Percival knew all about rapists. His sister had been attacked in Central Park by a guy they had caught. They had taken down his pants and what they did to humiliate and mark that black bastard would scar him for life. He was a black lecher with chronic satyriasis, the priest had told him. "And blacks are more sexual than we are and bigger there, too. So you shouldn't blame the guy." That had been ten years ago. Percival was going to really get even tonight with this guy who couldn't get enough of sex the right way.

"If you tell us now, nice and quiet, then we won't beat the shit out of you or nothing, right, boys?" It was Cluett, heavy arms all fat, thick thighs and calves, and a beer belly. Masters knew the kind, all bully.

"What did you say, sir?" he asked.

"You heard me," said Cluett, trying to talk chummy. "We all like a broad now and then. So out with it. Did you have real trouble with this woman? I mean did she let you, or did you have to use force? I mean the teeniest little bit of muscle?"

24

Masters stared at him, sensing a trap.

"If she cooperated with you . . . you know what I mean? . . . Like reacting, then, you'll get off. So describe it in detail." Cluett sat back and waited, breathing heavily. Masters stared at him. This Cluett must be a nut.

"If she helped you . . . sex-wise, then it isn't rape."

"I don't know what any of you are talking about," said Masters, as a slap from behind jerked his head forward to cut off his wind. Cluett came over to him, slouched over Masters's chair, and leaned into his ear. "Tell me. Go ahead. It won't get into the record. We see you're clean. Nothing on the yellow sheets. No record for nothin'. Not even a parking ticket. So now's your chance. Was she a good piece or not? Did she cooperate or just lie there?" The cop had his fist raised. Masters looked up and sniffled, pulling at his nostril with a free hand. The man behind Masters struck his head again and it slapped forward, hurting his neck vertebrae.

"No bruises!" warned a voice near the door. Cluett wanted to beat the hell out of the rapist. That's all they needed. After all the prostitutes had to offer, why would a guy get it off with force?

"What bruises?" the man behind Masters replied with great innocence. Masters's head went forward again. It was unbearable. He yelled in pain.

"Take off his shoes!" said Cluett, moving away in disgust. He had hoped for a vivid, rather sensational story of the rape. It made the details interesting. This guy, like all of them, would get off.

Masters sat barefoot and feeling very helpless. He never should've come here. He never should've left that job in the diner. New York—who needed it? Big-time, huh? Well, dammit, he had just big-timed himself into big trouble. And how the hell was he going to get ahold of his mother?

"What he means," someone was saying, while Masters cleared the faraway look from his eyes, "is that if you put it in, it's one thing. They call it penetration. It's the law. The girl has to prove it. We're on your side. Now if you put it in with her help only a little bit . . ." the cop held up two fingers . . . "then you're off scot-free. Right, boys?" They all nodded. "So tell us how was it?"

"You know you hit her plenty, to soften her up. You like to hit them, don't you?" It was Percival. Women resisted, that's what he knew. A woman liked a man, but only when she wanted it and not just when he did, which was anytime. That was a fact.

"Let's examine the guy . . . down there," suggested the man behind him. "We should do what they did to her, put him stark naked on a table with his legs spread and see whether he made it tonight. They did it to her, you know . . . rapist!"

How could anyone tell, wondered Masters. They were still pulling his leg. "And then we'll take a picture of him, too. Down there, like they done to her!"

"Were you at York and Sixty-first tonight?"

"I was at a movie."

"Where?"

"At a western."

"OK, so you're a cowboy, huh? Tough guy, huh?"

"Now tell us without no bullshit, Masters, can you tell us exactly where you were at 12:09 tonight?"

The cop who had been eating garlic and breathing in Masters's face stepped on his big toe. "Oops! Sorry. Meant to miss you."

26

"I seen a movie. Look, I think I got the stub." He fidgeted in his pockets and came out with one.

"I could use another glass of water."

While the men carefully inspected the theatre stub, another went for the water. He returned with a glass of yellow fluid. Masters took one look at it and shook his head.

"Don't want no water, big shot?" asked Percival.

Masters shook his head again. "It's not water. It's probably..."

"Probably what?" asked Cluett. "What is it?"

"Piss."

Percival took the glass. "Trouble with you sex freaks and degenerates is you get queer ideas about everything, even orange drink." He shook his head.

"Where was you after midnight, boy?"

"I left the movies and went to a bar on Second Avenue . . . I think."

His head got snapped for that one. "You think!" cried a voice. "Answer the man."

"Which bar? Did you meet a girl there? Did she ask you to fuck her? Did she take you to her place or what?"

"I want a lawyer. I can't talk to you about anything, not nothing until I get one . . . and you won't let me call my mother."

Masters was beginning to feel very sorry for himself.

They wouldn't let up on him. His voice took on a whine. He would tell his mom when he saw her. How these guys tortured him. What made them think he'd picked up a girl at a bar?

"It must have been near Joe's place. A lot of singles hang out there who want to get picked up and taken home. It's notorious for that."

"Write it like it happened," someone else was saying. Masters began to feel faint and sick, woozy, like he wasn't really there and it was a dream. He felt a pen being shoved between his fingers and saw a yellow pad down on the desk. It was school? No it wasn't, because there were men's voices ... He wanted some water, and Mom.

"Maybe we can start writing it for you, if you dictate it, boy," said the spokesman, Cluett. "Do your confession."

"I ain't going to write nothing. What do you guys think? I won't write nothing without a lawyer. How can I confess without a lawyer?"

"But you do 'confess' don't you? That's what you said, right?" The fat man had the look of a timber wolf, fat from a kill but still hungry. He leaned toward Masters, drilling him with his hateful eyes, and Masters felt like a dying man with coyotes around or vultures. He was strong, though. He'd get up and. . .

Someone clipped his left wrist and another hit him on the back of his neck again. He sank forward, nearly out.

"Supposing we draft it?" asked Allbright.

He started writing. He held a ball-point pen, looked down at the paper, then up again at the suspect. Masters looked out of it. Allbright supposed that with the effort of the rape and the reaction afterwards to being arrested and now this ... the guy wasn't all that big after all. Rapists weren't supermen!

Masters could feel them crowding in and he couldn't wake up. They began at his belt and started pulling his trousers down and laughing. Then someone asked him to drink this stuff which was warm and asked, "How was it? Good? Did you get it

28

off? You don't have to, you know, for the girl to cry rape." And then it got too hazy for him to see, only hear. The smell of sweat was overpowering and someone said, "Hey, confess, Masters! We ain't got all night."

He recalled going to a bar. Then another and another. Then the woman coming down the path and her first cry and how he had to hit her . . . and then later the screams in his ear as he left her. She had been scared. Not like his mother, who wasn't afraid of anything. She would have understood how uptight he had felt. He began to talk to her and tell her. "I didn't mean to hurt her, Mom. She was just a slut, a tramp."

And Mom listened. She nodded her head and said she understood, that he was her baby.

"They're taking his confession right now," Melo said to Bernard. "All of a sudden he started telling them. He started out with 'Yeah, I did a bad thing.' And he said he went to Joe's Bar. Must be Cartona's Bar and Grill."

At that moment the sergeant approached them.

"Sorry about this, but you two know the area. Your duty is the bar, Joe's place. You know Joe. Go see what you can find out. I should ask Detective Hemphill to do this, but he is taking a personal. We don't need the Rape Squad. He's confessed."

"Hemphill's always in the john when you want him the most," allowed Melo. "Okay, we'll go. Maybe he'll stand us a few."

"Don't forget we need evidence, Officer Bernard. Question Joe. We want to know was Masters in there. When and with whom, all that. Get us something the DA can live with in court, or we'll drop the charges

29

right now. The captain just told me. He's sick and tired of our being shot down all the time."

At Joe's Officers Bernard and Melo found the owner.

"Sit down so it don't look like I'm getting busted," he said.

He told them he had been closing up the night before last. He said there was this man, Ray Murray, lived over the bar. "Has a decorating business all over New York. He's rich. Well, he sees this guy moseying around down here. He calls the police. He sees this guy trying doors."

"What's the matter? What did he steal?" asked Melo.

"He didn't steal nothing."

They accepted beers. "He was prowling around," said Bernard, wishing to lead his man with a little more finesse than his partner. "Did you see him in here at all earlier, or the night before?"

"Him?"

"Yeah."

"That burglar."

"Only arrested one guy here lately, Joe. Yeah, him."

"I seen him!" Joe poured himself a drink from the tap and came back. The place was empty. He sat down.

"You did?" asked Bernard, pretending casualness. "When?"

"What's he been booked for?" asked Joe, intent on his beer.

"Attempted robbery. Breaking and entering . . . I don't know."

Melo knew Bernard would make detective if he kept it up like this. He was cool!

30

"Also," added Bernard slowly, "he raped a girl."

"Raped a girl!" Joe stood up, spilling his beer. "In here?"

"No, not in here, Joe. Down in that little park off the East River. They got his signed confession. He said he was here first; that he came back here to take a piss."

Joe didn't like being involved in sexual perversion. To him, rape was the worst crime in the world. Worse than murder. He went for three more beers.

"He gave us an X-rated version," said Bernard and followed Joe back to the beer tap. "None for me, thanks. He fucked her and buggered her."

"God!" said Joe, and let the beer foam over.

"You can say that again," said Bernard as quietly as his voice would allow.

"When I hear the sirens I look out my door and down next door to here. I see you guys arresting this bum. The guy trying to get in Ray Murray's place. Is that the one?"

"You seen him, alright."

"I seen him. He left here earlier. My john's busted. He said he had to take a leak. He had a cut."

"Over his eye?"

"Over his right eye."

The beer stood untouched before Bernard as he made notes.

"There was two girls standin' here."

"There were?"

"Yes, this guy with black hair, and big black eyebrows, he didn't notice them when they asked for a light.

"I went over and said, 'Say, mister, you gotta match for them girls?' He said no. Anyone with half an eye could see they was after a guy, but he didn't pay no attention. I said to her, 'Wait, I'll go get a

31

match.' When I come back, they had skipped. Left me with a five dollar tab. He was still here."

"Think, Joe. Is there anything he did that was suspicious or different?"

Joe thought, reached for the beer and drank it down. As the glass hit the counter he started speaking. "I got it!"

"What?"

"He was mumbling about his mother. He said things about him and some girl. Is that enough?"

"What things?"

"I couldn't hear exactly."

Bernard said no, that didn't count. "The girl lost a button from her blazer, they told me down at the station. The warrant stated that. It was torn off during the attack. It had a piece of cloth with it. Torn right out of the girl's blazer. In one piece. Button, cloth, and all."

"That's it!" Joe's eyes were wide.

"Okay, what's it?"

"I got the button."

"That there same button? No kiddin'?"

"With the cloth."

"You're shittin' us!" said Melo.

"This guy had it in his hand. Was playing with it, looking at it, rolling it around in his hand like one of them fetish pieces. Like in that movie with Humphrey Bogart, wasn't it?"

"No, it wasn't," said Melo. "It was Kirk Douglas."

"Where's this button now?" asked Bernard.

"He left here looking to take a leak, I guess, or to break in Murray's door. He walked outside and left it on the bar. I picked it up. Thought first he'd left me a tip. It was gold. I didn't see the cloth until I picked it up."

"And?" breathed Bernard and Melo in unison.

"I thrown it in the garbage."

Two hours later, with five cans to inspect, they were still out back in the alley, down to their shorts to preserve their uniforms, wallowing in garbage. The two men had gone through stale onions and spinach, tomato sauce, which left pink stains on Melo's skinny legs, old bread and napkins, and other totally unrecognizable food. Bernard was doing fine. He was working the fruit and vegetable pile with a white kerchief tied across his nose. He was up to his elbows in decaying lettuce when he let out a yelp.

"I found it!" It was hard and flat and about the size of a quarter. He wiped it off, and he knew he had his evidence.

Melo smiled, washed his legs and arms with a small hose, and reached for his jacket. Bernard pulled on his pants.

They sped back to the station house.

"A guy like that shouldn't be allowed to walk the streets and threaten the lives and morals of our women," said Melo. "His mind on sex like that must be sick . . . don't you think? And he don't look like no Don Juan, does he?"

"He's sick," said Paul Bernard. "Real sick."

Bernard knew that button would put the rapist away for twenty-five years—it connected him with his victim like a chain. This rape case would go forward.

Three

Guy Masters was thirty-two years old and, according to statistics, too old for rape. Even though he had confessed to it, in his mind it hadn't happened. It was as if somebody had planned it all, had set him up. Somebody had fixed it to get him in jail, somebody who hated him.

Finally, late last night after they had finished with him, one of the cops said he could call his mother. She would never believe it, that he had done what they said, and she would come to fix it right. They had taken him to the Tombs then, just as it was getting light, and he had slept a few hours in a cell with five other guys.

The guys were crazy, mixed-up, and they said they didn't belong here either. The next morning one kept saying how long he'd been there. "I been in the Tombs for a year. I ain't seen my Legal Aid in three weeks. They keep delaying my trial and I'm innocent. I didn't kill nobody."

34

"Justice delayed is justice denied," said his friend, a man who identified himself as "once a lawyer."

"Brandeis said that," he confided to Masters, trying to gain status. "They keep you here 'til you rot like the Count of Monte Cristo."

Then he had gone before a judge who had set bond, and then, handcuffed, he had been taken back to the station for a lineup. He had gone through it all in a daze, waiting for his mother to come and rescue him. When they brought him back to the Tombs, Masters sat on a bench, his mind turned off. He could learn to do this, like an animal in a stable. He would just eat, sleep, and not think until he was safe again, until Mom came to get him out. He figured he could handle it. He could wait.

But he hadn't figured on the night, the overwhelming silence. Unlike the tranquil days, the night was explosive. It carried the constant threat of annihilation. Something unknown, unseen, was after him. Something was out there that he couldn't see, and he was defenseless against it. Masters crouched up against the wall of the cell, trembling and terrified, and waited for the morning to come. He would get out, he would have to get out. He couldn't take the nights in here.

Next morning, he was led upstairs to the room where they said his lawyer would meet him. His first question when he saw an old and impressive man was, "How much will it cost?"

"Don't worry, Guy, your mother is taking care of that."

Sturdevant Warren, attorney-at-law, had seen better days and this day was one of his worst. First, he was nursing a slight hangover from wine; second, he had decided to accept once-despised rape cases.

Actually this was his first, though he had been tempted before, but the guys at the chess club had been asking him lately what case he was on, and "how is the old law." He hadn't had one to tell them about since the civil liberties thing he did years ago with Arthur Garfield Hays, Henry Van Veen, and John Finnerty. Then they kept after him to retell how he and Roger Baldwin had done it during World War I when the "old legal fox had been the first draft dodger" and "now look at 'em all. You see 'em in Sweden so many years after the war and in Canada, and, Sturdevant, you wonder how they can just leave house and home and 'go native' somewhere else."

"Sturdy," as his older friends called him, from when he was that tall and had played first base at Harvard, was six-feet-two but bent over at sixty-eight. His wild white hair was washed before his court appearance, flying back from his strong, assertive face. He looked like a man who couldn't be coerced or intimidated. And it helped to be tall when on stage before judges and juries.

Nature had endowed Sturdevant Warren with a leaning toward vacations. He had always indulged himself, and when he finished a case, his buddies wouldn't see him until the fees ran out. Then he would reappear, to their admonitions that he ought to salt it away, not spend it in Vegas or living it up at Boca Raton.

They had been right. When he'd cashed his last war bond, clipped the last clipping from the bonds left him by a father who had gambled and had been elected mayor up in New England, he had become frightened for the first time in his life.

Lately, the subject of rape had become of deep concern to society. Women were all up in arms about it, now that they considered themselves "equal."

They acted like rape was something new, cooked up by male chauvinist pigs. Well, rape was as old as time—it was so old you might even consider it "natural."

"Man takes what he wants!" Sturdy had said often. "And that's why they need lawyers. I see a bright future for an expert in the crime of rape."

"Admirable," his cronies had said, smiling and proud. "You're going to see to it that women get protection. Perhaps you'll have to do with changing laws?"

"On the contrary. I'm going to defend the man."

And now he was doing it. Too many men were called rapists. Old hat. It was traditional. Women always lured the man. Streets filled with them. Enticement? Yes! Rape? Hell, no! Man was only doing his thing. You couldn't blame a red-blooded man the way things were, anyway. Proliferation of sex books, X-rated films, pictures of nude women, massage parlors. Why a guy didn't have a chance. And everyone knows women love to be raped . . . fantasize about it, in fact. That's what he told his cronies. He believed men were being falsely charged. He'd take the next rape case he was offered, although God knows most rapists couldn't afford his fee! And he had. A fellow named Masters. Guy Masters. His mother was Leila McMurtry from Boston. He'd known that family. Leila had married into the rich set, late, after her kids were nearly grown. And the old guy had croaked and left her a bundle. A fee of five thousand would be easy, and costs, later. He, Sturdevant Warren, would represent his first rapist and let the press know he was back in the saddle. He walked into the visitors room at the Tombs with his heart beating a little too fast. Better watch the wine and cigars. Young Dr. Prutting knew medicine, and had warned him.

Warren was confident, but he wasn't quite prepared for the ugly, heavily browed young man sitting there sniveling, wiping at his nostril like a prizefighter whose nose had been knocked to pieces. He was big, menacing, and somehow he didn't seem too bright. My God, he looked like a rapist!

Warren decided to treat him to a series of blows to let him know how dangerous his case was, and how close he could come to jail without him.

"So, she paid you, eh? When is she coming down?"

"She did, and she's not," said Warren. "She's leaving on a cruise. It was all planned in advance and I told her to go ahead and enjoy herself, that I'd have you out in no time, on bond anyway. She called me right after the cops called her. She said she'd write to you. Don't worry, she wired the money before she left."

Master's face was incredulous. "You mean she's not coming? She's not coming to see me?" His black eyes filled with tears, and he stared at Warren like a lost child.

But Sturdevant Warren had no time for a momma's boy. "Listen Masters," he said. "I'm the one who's going to get you out of here. She paid me to do it, and I'm going to.

"If she hadn't, son, you could stand trial for ninety years or be sentenced to death. You are in a hell of a lot of trouble. Don't you know it?"

Masters shrugged. Didn't she know it?

Warren assumed his most arrogant air. "Don't think because a couple of rapists got off with jail sentences instead of the death penalty on a Supreme

Court decision you can now go out and knock off some innocent girl and go scot-free. You may be put away for good! So don't act smart with me. Since you have already confessed to rape, tell me about it. Keep your voice low, because they plant stoolies here to listen, and talk straight to me. I'm the only thing going for you right now. You confeoood!"

Masters sobered. "I was offered another lawyer but I didn't take him. A Legal Aid guy. I hung in there for Mom to help. I knew she would come through."

"Well, we've got to get you out of here . . . out on bail. The only people who stay in here are vagrants, people with no family, no jobs or roots. You got roots. What happened to you in the court yesterday?"

"I can tell you. But I don't think the judge could."

Masters obviously was ready to dramatize his position, a device known to Warren. "I doubt it. But why?"

"He was asleep. They listed a lot of trumped-up charges like I was Attila the Hun or the Boston Strangler. This judge asks me, 'How do you plead?' I says, 'I didn't do none of them things . . . burglary, attempted burglary and all that.' He says, 'So you plead not guilty?' and I says, 'Yes.' Then he says, 'Put it down for the day after tomorrow.' That's tomorrow."

Warren wasn't giving a course in amateur law. "What did he set the bail at?"

"Fifty thousand."

"Like you were the latest sky-jacker. I'll get you out on bail. What happened after they set bail?"

"I was put in a lineup like a criminal. I guess it was her out there. They made me walk out against this white wall with them lines on it. But the room was dark. I couldn't see."

"You're practically put away now—what with that confession and rape tests she probably took. She was probably out there pointing at you. I don't think she's stupid."

Masters smiled. Big white strong teeth . . . black brows . . . not the smile of an animal but that of a man who had been denied protection all his life—a man who now had it and was glad deep down to his toes.

"I tried to reach Mom in Boston several times— two, three times—I kept getting a busy signal."

"You never spoke to her and she was the person you said you wanted to speak with? You know that business about the telephone call is to permit an accused man to get legal assistance. Your mom called me."

"I never got to make my call. They beat me."

"Look, you're in real trouble. I can't get you off entirely. Maybe a plea-down. That confession is tough to beat. About your rights, though. Did they read them to you?"

"I guess so. They said they did."

"Did they or didn't they?"

"Whatever the cop read from that card, he read fast. How do I know what the guy said to me?"

"Fast, eh?"

"Yeah, fast."

"What did they do to you at the station?"

"They shoved me down in a chair under a light."

"Over your head? The top of your skull?"

Masters looked at him sharply. "Yeah. That's right."

"It was hot. And burned into your brain?"

"Like an iron."

"You got a headache and became very thirsty?"

"Yeah. I got a headache. A terrible one. I was very thirsty."

"Did they bring you some water?"

"Yeah, but it was hot . . . boiling hot. I guess they thought it was funny. I spit it out. My tongue is still burnt."

"How long did they subject you to this . . . er, torture?"

"Right away after they brought me some piss to drink."

"Piss? You mean . . . urine?"

Masters nodded. From under his brows his eyes searched for pity. Warren made a note on his pad.

"Then they all left. I was there with them an hour. Then I guess it was three hours I was left alone after that."

"How do you know how long it was?"

"This big clock tickin' on the wall over the poster of the Dodge sheriff."

"Was it hot or cold—stuffy or breezy?"

"They had this light on over my head. I got up an' moved my chair from under it. There was no window. It got very hot. Then they came back. More of them than before. They began. . ."

"To beat you?"

"Not . . . really . . . beat."

"Did they use a hose, do things that wouldn't leave marks?"

"This guy started slammin' my head around. He said it wouldn't leave no marks or bruises but it hurt. The guy said, 'No bruises, now.' And the other guy said, 'Hell, this won't leave no bruises,' but it still hurts all up and down my neck and back here."

Warren walked around and looked. "We'll have a competent doctor look at it and make a report. We'll get X-rays and testimony. I'm sorry."

Masters looked surprised at his concern. "Oh,

that's alright. They shouldn't ought to do that, should they, Mr. Warren?"

"But they do. They got your confession that way."

Masters looked surprised, then agreed. "Yes, they did, didn't they?"

"Did you rape that girl?"

Masters just looked at him for a moment. "I don't remember too much about that night."

"You did pretty well on how much they tortured you."

"How could I forget?"

"The episode with the girl couldn't have impressed you very much, then?"

"What do you mean?" His "Who, me?" look was back.

"Did you have a willing girl on your hands? Was Susan Landress an old girl friend? Had you known her before?"

"Who's Susan Landress?"

"The girl you confessed to raping. The girl who put the finger on you in the dark. That's who she is."

Warren couldn't imagine a man doing what his client had confessed to without having strong impressions later, even though he had been drinking. According to what he had learned from a short briefing from a doctor who had testified at three rape cases, "In about twenty percent of the time both parties had been drinking . . . but alcohol is not necessary to the rape."

He had been handed a book, too, that said "white women are more vulnerable to rape, when drinking or drunk with a man, than blacks."

"You were drinking . . . there's a clear association between rape and drinking; so out with it . . . had you?"

"Not much. I don't remember."

"How about the victim ... er, the girl. Did she cooperate? I mean in ... the act?"

Warren wanted to establish the man was not responsible for his act ... that the girl and he had been drinking, were friends. "After you may have been drinking with her, and went off with her, like singles do, what happened? I'd like to know for your sake."

"For me? Why?"

"If she's a fighter, which I suspect she is, we'll have trouble. If not, I may ask her to answer a lot of different questions about her past. So if she knows all about sex and did certain things while you raped her, I can tell. If she didn't but just lay there, then that's different. I'll figure she's near a virgin."

"She weren't no virgin ..." Masters began, then realized he had been tricked and shut up.

Warren pretended he hadn't observed the slip and asked, "Why?"

"I guess from the way she rushed to the police to tell them what happened. I mean, she must have been raped before."

"How do you know what she reported?"

"They said I was 'brutal and vicious,' that I bit her and ripped off her blouse, and buggered her."

"She obviously didn't make it up. She must know about such things. You're right. She's not a virgin."

"It was all like a dream, Mr. Warren. I got to tell you that much. A man came through the room and told them to break it up."

"Why did you sign the confession?"

"I don't remember even seeing it or signing it."

That was just what he wanted. A client who had been beaten into submission, then into a confession, and who would testify to police brutality.

43

"I'll be back. I've got more to ask you." Warren hurried out before the traffic rush. He knew there was a confession, but he didn't know exactly what was in it. He knew the police had probably over-stepped themselves when they hadn't let his client make a telephone call, had used undue force and duress, and hadn't properly advised him of his rights. Therefore, the confession could probably be thrown out. He didn't want to put Masters on the stand at all, even if he could use him to prove the confession had been extorted under pressure.

He would have to investigate this girl, Susan Lan-dress. All young women had lovers and what with promiscuous sex and the free-wheeling style of sin-gles, he'd prove she was a hippie. Who would believe she could be raped?

He must get a detective to do a little research on her, before and after the "prelim."

Four

Patricia was tired. She had been preparing for the series day and night and now at the very moment when she needed all her physical and mental strength, the subject of rape seemed to pull her under, like quicksand. "Maybe it's too broad a subject. The scripts read just fine, Joe, but I can't really cover the subject without going back and starting with the English Common Law."

"You'll be 'on the air' for the next ten years, baby," he had responded. "Take as long as you think it requires."

"Well, here goes," she sighed and plunged into the script before her.

"Rape is a sexual offense. It breaches the mores or customs of society and human experience for as far back as can be found in recorded law." She hesitated a moment, then looked directly into the camera. Firmly, deliberately, she recited the facts:

"We all know what rape is. It is a crime, a felony, in

which a man forces a woman into sexual relations against her will. It is a crime which men commit against women. Men rape, women are their victims. And at a time when more and more women are rebelling against sex-object roles in this society, more and more men seem brutally intent upon reducing them to the most vulnerable objects possible. Two hundred thousand rapes will take place this year in the United States. One every fifteen minutes. In fact, while many crimes are decreasing in number, the crime of rape is on the increase. Forcible rape is up 40.5 percent this year. In one of the months covered by FBI crime index, it was up 90.3 percent.

"So, men, this is not simply a Women's Liberation issue drummed up by a bunch of man-hating broads. It is an incredibly serious problem, a problem which threatens you, your wives, your daughters, your mothers.

"Fifty thousand rapes were reported last year, but officials believe that number represents only 25 percent of all the rapes committed. Why didn't those other women report their rapes? Why didn't they call the police?

"They were embarrassed, they were ashamed, they were humiliated. They wanted to go home and take a bath and forget about what had happened to them. But that's only part of the reason. When we take a look at the laws concerning rape, we can see clearly why women don't report this crime. They don't want to go through the ordeal of PROVING they have been raped. The burden of guilt, ladies and gentlemen, is on the victim, not her attacker.

"The victim must prove that she did not consent to the rape. Establishing consent as an element in rape has always involved the extent of resistance and the

46

extent of force used by the victim to resist. She must meet her attacker with what is legally termed 'earnest resistance.' Rape reaches far back into English Common Law, but the word essentially means 'the unlawful ravishing of a woman against her will and without her consent or under circumstances in which her capacity or power to express her volition has been inhibited, nullified, or has been proven nonexistent.'

"If you are wondering why my speech suddenly became filled with long, strange legal words, it's because I am reading from a book entitled *Criminal Law in New York.*

"Why so much emphasis in the law on the victim's role? Why must she prove how strongly she resisted? Well, it's a simple answer, and a chilling one, and it's the reason why most women don't report rape:

"THE LAW DOESN'T TRUST WOMEN. RAPE LAWS ARE DESIGNED BY MEN TO PROTECT MEN FROM THE UNFAIR ACCUSATIONS OF WOMEN.

"The legendary male belief that the woman is a seducer—that she leads the naturally aggressive man on beyond his point of control and then cries 'rape'—is embodied in our law!

"Too many people think of rape as a laughable, forgivable crime, that if a woman wished to, she could avoid it. That the woman actually loves rape from the hands of a he-man rapist, and that she not only invites the attack but enjoys it!

"Speaking as a woman ..." Patricia drew in her breath as the camera drew back—"I simply state 'rubbish.' Rape is a nightmare to women, and nothing is more threatening or frightening. Women are deeply concerned about it, from here to California. Shame, humiliation, and man's disregard for a woman's feel-

47

ings have won over during these many years. The emotional experience of rape could never be understood by a man. This emotional experience and its consequences, should the victim choose to go to the law for help, are followed by such humiliation to her, as a female, that she won't even report it. The pity of all this is that the 200,000 women marked for rape in these United States this coming year will receive little help from a system which has traditionally treated them as the guilty one and let the rapist go free."

A close-up. "Patricia Rankin. Group One News. More on rape next Monday at this time."

She was shaken up when she finished. Angry. When it was all laid out, it was so incredibly unfair. Sometimes it seemed to her that women didn't have a chance, that all the cards were stacked against them.

"But I broke out," she thought. "I made it. I'm tough."

Congratulations met her on her way to the dressing room.

"Nice going!"

"Some beginning. How can you carry it?"

"I'll have to use more makeup under your eyes next time. But God, is that a heavy subject!"

She closed the door on them.

Yes, it was an exciting subject. But the facts had begun to sicken her. You couldn't celebrate rape with wine and friends. Patricia decided to duck the after-work cocktails. She hurried, knowing they would all meet in front of her door, for she was always the last one to be ready. Outside, she hailed a cab and went directly home.

There, looking out over Central Park and the Lincoln Center area, she saw three hundred acres of woods, lakes, and paths and knew that in that park right then someone was being attacked and hopefully "resisting to her utmost."

She took a sleeping pill and lay down to stare at the ceiling. Before she fell asleep she had reached a conclusion. She would put a rape victim on her program. She would protect her identity. No one but a woman who had been raped could tell the story the way it should be told.

Susan wasn't used to living indoors. Even though Anne Treadwell had made the studio apartment seem less like living in a shoe box, she found herself sitting near the window rather than on the king-sized sofa bed with its fluffy pillows. There she could watch singles gather on the sidewalk in front of Friday's, a popular Second Avenue restaurant. The view wasn't much other than that, for the tall apartment houses all around cut off the sun and whatever breeze might have come from the East River. Lately, ever since coming back from that interrogation at the district attorney's office, she had felt as if she was on a treadmill and couldn't get off.

"If you come in here and swear a guy raped you, miss," the man who had taken her deposition had warned, "you'd better be prepared."

Then he had told her what her chances were. Her chances? It was as if she had done something. "Get a job if you don't have one. Don't move around in singles groups or get into any weird life-style here," he had warned. "This isn't the kind of place where surfboard riders and swingers get believed when the jury hears them say they've been raped."

Inside her all-white studio, Susan stared out the window, half listening to a TV news report while

Anne raced around the room in a last minute panic trying to get too many things into a small shoulder bag.

Their supper together had been meager, but they had laughed and talked. Anne wasn't the most exciting person in the world, but it was better than being alone, and somehow she realized how much Susan wanted to belong.

"I'm going now," Anne had said at the door, before throwing a kiss. "I'll be gone 'til next Thursday, then home for ten days. I'll get caught up on all your little hangups. Use whatever you want of mine. Goodby."

Anne didn't know about her being raped, yet.

Being a victim of a criminal attack made one a complainant and a witness, too. There was no one else for the law people to begin with. She suddenly realized that if she just quietly disappeared and let it drop, the charges and all, she wouldn't disappoint anyone, least of all those men down in the DA's office. She would be letting that nice Julia McElroy down, maybe. But then again she had made it plain that Susan was on her own.

"Get yourself a nice job and a steady boyfriend. I'm going away soon," she had said. "So hang in there. I'm so sorry . . . about all that's happened."

Get a job. That's what people were telling her, as if she expected to live off them. Well, tomorrow she was going to. The British-based employment agency's ad was lying on the blue throw rug beneath her, and as she sat on the floor by the window, she read it again.

WE HAVE PLACED NICE GIRLS
ALL OVER THE WORLD.
WHEN YOU SAY YOU'RE FROM NELSON'S
THEY SAY
"YOU'RE HIRED!"

The next morning, running a comb through her

hair, she thought about the job. She made up her mind today would be the last day she would feel trapped by what had happened. She had to break loose, and belong here.

She put on a simple skirt, a blouse, a lightweight sweater, and appraised herself in the mirror. She looked fresh, clean, nice. She didn't look like the kind of girl who had been raped. She didn't look like a "slut." But just to be sure, she wiped off her lipstick, and wadded the tissue into her purse as she left.

"Go north until you get to East Sixty-second Street and Second. Got it? That's East Sixty-second and Second," the woman at the employment agency had told her. "The ad agency is in a small brownstone. Just run up the stairs and you'll see a bell. It isn't a bell, really. It activates this gong. Anyway, they'll know it's you. They need a girl to type things right away. You won't disappoint us, will you? You'll be there, right? Ask for Michael Rose; he's the owner."

When the door opened, she saw a man who resembled a jellybean, in shirtsleeves, and with a wide round smile, a lot of teeth, and just the straggly remnants of black hair.

"You're the girl from Nelson's, aren't you? I hope so. You're our type."

She liked him immediately. Without waiting, he backed in and said, "Follow me." Michael Rose was too fat to look hip, but he tried. His bell-bottoms bulged at the wrong places, and his fat breasts showed through his printed knit shirt.

Inside a small office with shelves on all four walls, she was ordered to sit down. The shelves were a mass of photographs, some curled with age, others half-pulled from their mailing covers. All of them were of most attractive girls.

Looking her over carefully and ending at her face,

he said, "We're a boutique. We do everything. Just everything. We take it from the beginning and go all the way to the end, whether it's an ad, a TV commercial, or just a part of it. We do the graphics, the copy, or the whole package."

She nodded, feeling humble and small-townish. He was dynamic, sure of himself, aggressive. Perhaps this man, in his forties, was New York. At least he looked Madison Avenue, and he acted tough. As he spoke, his pudgy fingers grasped at the air and then balled into a fist to pound the desk. Ashtrays, filled to overflowing with old butts, bounced when he thumped the old desk.

"How tall are you, Miss Landers?"

"Landress," she said. "L-A-N-D-R-E-S-S."

"It's Flemish, isn't it? I knew from the start. You're five-seven, right? You could actually model later if you wanted to, like in all the top fashion magazines. This is Thursday. I don't see girls today. Mostly this place is awash with girls trying to get in here on what they call 'go sees.' That means they go and I see."

She watched him carefully. Did he mean that some day she might get to be a model for one of the ads? She realized it was something a lot of kids on the beach thought was glamorous. She had read all the books. New York didn't just offer this stuff to you.

His black, beady eyes stared right into hers as he talked, as if he was totally interested in her, Susan Landress, a little girl from California. He went on talking, hypnotic and dominating. When he had finished, she knew what the agency was, that it had ten people, and that it would be big some day soon. She felt certain he knew what he was talking about.

At the door she told him, "It's very exciting. I hope I get the job. I'd be totally committed."

52

"But you do have the job. You do." Then he told her to report for work the next morning. "I'm too involved today with new suntan lotion meetings."

The tape of Sonny and Cher stopped, and he took a long last look at her. She heard girls laughing in a back room, someone coughing, and a voice say, "Son of a bitch!"

Mike Rose laughed, "They're all nuts. Artists, you know."

As she walked downtown, she realized she had met someone who would be totally unbelievable to most of her friends in Santa Monica. Out there people worked to live—here they seemed to live for their work. She figured that Rose's enthusiasm was already wearing off on her. He would give her a place to hang her hat, become an individual and a participant, too. She'd stay in New York, face whatever the end of the tunnel promised, and be strong about it. Then when Anne came back, and she had the companionship of a girl who traveled from world capitol to world capitol, she'd begin to broaden her mind. It would be good.

Eight days later, Anne came back. Susan told her that in those few days she had moved up from steno to executive secretary.

She wasn't prepared for jealousy.

"What exactly do you do that earns you two hundred a week?"

"I do about everything imaginable, darling," Susan said. "We take it from the concept and build it. We create it and then see it through. From the graphics to when it happens." She knew she was parroting Mike, but who could really say it better?

"What's 'it'?" asked Anne with a bite in her voice.

She was standing before the full length mirror, rubbing herself down with a heavy towel.

Anne said, "You keep saying 'it.' What's 'it'?"

"What do you mean?" Susan answered, trying to get a last look at herself before going off. It was late and Mike would be mad. Damn Anne for hogging the mirror. "What do you mean?" She was asking questions twice, too. She'd better check herself on that.

"It! You take 'it' and you shape 'it' and you make 'it' happen. What's 'it'?"

"'It' is the idea, darling. The thing that will sell the product to the public. It's up to Mike and us to get it and once we have it, my dear, then it's all the way."

Anne turned on her. She frowned, tall and dark and completely absorbed in what she was saying. "You know, Susan, you'd better watch yourself. You're beginning to be affected the least bit and it sounds awful! You're overworking phrases like the devil. So, catch some good shows, see other people, take in a concert or an opera. If we get time this weekend, we should go to a group discussion or rap session to broaden your scope. In the meantime, stop saying 'darling'."

When Anne had gone, Susan had a chance at the mirror and seriously thought over what she had been told. Maybe Anne was right. My God, this place was complex. Her mother had told her to marry a nice boy and settle down to making babies and creating things in lace like her ancestors from the old country. But things in New York weren't all that easy. She took a big breath and walked up the street to the office feeling clean and healthy and tougher than she ever thought she could be.

At six that night Rose came dashing in, sweating and holding a photo dripping wet in his hands yelling, "Count on working late tonight. This shot stinks!"

All day he had been using the back studio, supervising tests for the new suntan campaign. The oil company management for Tan-up had suddenly reacted to the old slogan which said, "Look like a native. Use Tan-Up," stating in a sharp memo that Mike had better stop downing the minorities through their space and come up with something that didn't make the company seem anti-native or lily-white, either, for that matter.

She sat waiting for Mike reading back issues of *Vogue* and wondering when he would want her. She made a call to the apartment at seven o'clock to find that Anne was still out.

Mike soon came in and threw himself in his big overstuffed chair. The psychedelic light was on and he just stared at it. "Shit!" he said finally.

She felt sorry for him. "What is it?"

He looked at her as if seeing her for the first time. "You could do it, damn it. You could do it." He jumped up, took her by the hand, and said, "Follow me."

He led her into the small all-white studio in back. They were alone. The place was a mess. Cameras in every corner, all lights on, empty glasses, coffee containers, and butts scattered all over stools and camp chairs. "Sit down."

She did. He went to the huge paper roll suspended from the ceiling and drew it down. It spread twelve feet wide and twenty feet across the room. "Now go in there, put on that bikini, and come out. And for God's sake don't step on the paper with your feet. I'm going to make a beach scene shot with you."

Caught up in his frenzy, happy to be pleasing him, Susan stripped and pulled on the bikini briefs and adjusted the bra.

By the time she'd completed her makeup and wiped

her feet clean in the wash and dried them, the music tape was on and the lights in the studio had been adjusted, focused on the center of the stage.

"Lie down on your back on the paper and take a big breath," he said without looking at her. In Mike's hand was his Leica. She did as he asked. The lights were hot. She waited and began to perspire.

"Not that way!" He came over and moved her legs so that one knee was bent. Then he combed her hair so that it fell all over the white paper under her. "Nice. Nice and easy. Relax, like that. Darling, that's wonderful. Now stand up—yes, that's it, and slowly turn. Good, you're on a merry-go round, darling, and it's moving ever so slowly, like that." As he spoke, she could hear the snapping shutter and she felt better, gained confidence. He was so very good at this. Everyone said so.

"Now slowly bend down ... feet apart a little. You're supple, oh so very, very supple like a reed and you're bending down to put some of the oil from your finger tips on your knee caps. No, not like that, like this."

He came to her and brushed at her knees. She did as he directed. But he didn't step back. She straightened up. He was near her and she suddenly felt very vulnerable and sexy. It had never occurred to her before that Mike was anything more than a boss.

He put out a hand and caressed her shoulder.

"Here, put lotion here ... and then ease your finger tips down beneath your bra a little, like this."

The music swelled and the room began turning and Susan suddenly felt nauseous. She wouldn't faint. She just wouldn't.

His fingertips were away from her breasts and he kept snapping pictures while she turned, bent, and swayed. She fairly floated to the dreamy music, entirely caught up. She felt like a gorgeous, sexy wild woman. She could be a model, a star.

Suddenly the music went dead and he was pressing against her. His eyes were cloudy and he was saying something sharp with what seemed like anger. "Take it off. I want some shots of you entirely nude."

She didn't breathe or move.

"All the girls go through it at first. *Vogue* and *Harper's* ads are what I'm talking about. You'll get two hundred an hour from the client. You'll be a sensation!" His eyes moved up and down. She moved back instinctively from something threatening her. She didn't know what to do. He walked away and she saw him get under a big black cloth behind a large camera. His voice was muffled and thick.

"What's a few inches of cloth? I can tell now what you look like without 'em. So, darling, strip the bikini off like I want."

Susan's head was suddenly clear. "Sorry, Mike. Not me." Her reaction had been automatic. "But that's it."

Out he came, his eyes red, his face flushed.

"If you can't hang loose any better than that about a little nudity and some fun when I'm up-tight and in a jam financially, then you'd better look for another job beginning right now, darling. Get it all on and go!"

She froze.

She couldn't speak. She had lost her job!

"Your shorthand stinks, too," he said.

She could hardly dress for the tears. Then she ran into the hallway and down the stairs. At the bottom she remembered her purse and turned to go back.

There he stood holding her purse by the draw string.

"I forgot my purse," she said.

"Here!" He tossed it at her. She caught it. Then she saw him make a sudden move and a quarter dance through the air. "This is a tip, darling. A tip from me that you'll never, never make it in New York. You haven't got the creative urge. The thing. It will never get together for you!" He walked away.

She went into the street, saw the crowd at Friday's breaking up, and walked on to her apartment wondering about herself. She was worried. What was wrong with her?

Maybe Mike was right and maybe Anne was right, too. She had been too sure of herself, overconfident. What right had she to think that she could beat New York at its own game?

With a deep sigh, she pushed the elevator button and watched the door close. As she did, a man wearing workmen's clothes came through the street door and began looking at name plates of the persons living in the building. But Susan was too overwrought to notice him.

Five

D. P. Scott, short for Donald Paulson Scott, was an Assistant District Attorney. He had the worst office of anyone on the DA's staff, with peeling paint, poor ventilation, and a view of the backside of another building. But for twenty-eight years he had worked in that stuffy office, and worked hard. He was the DA's expert in sexual offense cases.

The dirt, and the law in which he was involved, had so sickened him and darkened his outlook that he had lost all sense of humor, and the only thing he looked forward to was retirement.

He was tall, yet appeared smaller, with a hollow chest and intense cough. A few grey hairs, a pair of glasses slipping down his small nose made him appear kindly and old, yet his scorching memos sent juniors scurrying for the law books, anxious for his approval. Scott was an inside terror. But he would never be famous elsewhere.

Today the old bachelor was troubled as he watched

the air conditioner stir up dust on the books which were tumbled about near his swivel chair. Fred Michaels, his new man, would be coming here in a few minutes to discuss the Landress rape. Michaels was thirty and the sort of man D. P. remembered himself to be at that age. With his lifetime experience of judging men at a glance, he had selected Michaels from a dossier after a handshake.

He fingered the crumbling cover of a book on charges and ran over in his computer mind what he knew about Frederick Osborne Michaels.

Thirty, single, graduate of Fordham Law School magna cum laude, second-string football, second-string basketball. Born under Throg's Neck Bridge in The Bronx. Father a police captain. Hobby: law and order. Loves: the logic of law, photography, sailing, surfing. Ambition: to be criminal judge in a high court, to marry a girl who likes the outdoors. Voted by class: "Most handsome grind in school." Appearance: eager, shy, fast-moving, quick speech. Drives too fast, smokes too much, talks too much. Wholly affable. Score: (in Scott's mind) "Wish he were the son I didn't have." Now this educated man who was wholly devoted to the law would be assigned to him to handle the next rape case which could be expected any hour today.

It was a crime on the rise and one in which the Women's Liberation Movement's activists had shown increasing interest. "Sex between today's women and men is rape" said one of them on the air yesterday.

And they got away with it. Reasoning: Women have no choice when a husband or lover makes his chauvinistic demand. Be raped or be damned. "We submit. We have submitted. But no more."

Frederick Michaels would have to be more than

super—more than magna cum laude—to prove facts in court before a jury made up of members of a submissive society brainwashed to believe any miniskirted, liberal-minded, healthy specimen of womanhood was looking for the ultimate relationship.

His intercom exploded in crackles. "Frederick Michaels to see you." D.P.'s mind came down to earth and the matter of facts facing them both . . . the first interview in which he, Scott, would set the tenor of their entire relationship.

He stood in the doorway. Tall, six feet, thin, with a full head of sandy hair and a rangy look. He came in like a man with a purpose, loping across the room in one step, bent low to take the outstretched hand. He had a shy kind of grin, like that of a modest but self-assured man.

"Finally," he said, "I meet you!" He seemed genuinely excited and pleased. He sat down at D.P.'s wave of the hand. One glance and D.P. knew the man would impress a judge and jury with his air of sincerity and honesty. He began slowly, taking Michaels down through the state's legal history, pointing out the points of evidence which had to be proven.

"Conviction depends upon proving resistance with earnestness and to the victim's utmost. You have to prove penetration, 'no matter how slight,' and you have to prove identity 'beyond a shadow.' Corroboration is fine if you have it."

"What about our new rape law? I know we don't need corroboration. . . ." His grin told Scott he already had answered his own question. "But I do presume that no good attorney would fail to bring in as much evidence as was available . . . that no DA would take a rape case—even now—without a preponderance of

61

evidence—that while the corroboration of a witness may not be necessary anymore to prove rape, it will impress a jury—and the judge."

"We never took a vow in this department to suppress evidence or to overlook testimony which would help convict. We're still going for all the corroboration possible to clinch a rape case. The new state law was set up to make it easier to win a rape case, not to lose one by ignoring valuable evidence which can aid in the conviction of a suspect."

Then Scott took him down the list of landmark cases which set the opinions in the state. "And one of the ironies is that the witness or complainant/witness can be villified and investigated publicly, can be stripped of her decency, and her past exposed whether that past had anything to do with the crime being charged by her or not—while the suspect, even though he may have been tried for rape ten times, can not be subjected to the same digging. In fact, damn it, his prior convictions on rape are not even admissible evidence unless he takes the stand."

Fred was impressed by the man's vehemence.

"Rape isn't like other crimes," Fred offered. "I don't relate it to murder—except that, as Dr. Karl Menninger states, 'Rape is less a sexual act than a form of assault and mayhem—a form of hurting, debasing, and destroying another person for power drive satisfaction.' He calls it 'a sin.'"

Scott looked back at him and slowly relit an already half-smoked pipe, letting the smoke curl and grow near the ceiling. He knew Michaels was trying to impress him with his study of rape. Well, he had succeeded.

"*People* v. *Masters* is yours," Scott said, and handed him the packet. "We have too few assistant

DA's in this town to expect you to see it from start to finish, yet you might do so, if you request it. We've depleted the New York Police Department. More than 1,500 cops are off the street helping in arrest procedures and we still need 200 more courtrooms. Nonetheless, despite the calendar and the pressure, I'd like to put this guy away. This time no plea-downs, no acceptance of a lesser plea to criminal assault. We have his confession!"

Two days later Fred told his boss he'd read the confession.

"They'll charge it was forced," he said. "We have witnesses. Julia McElroy, and the cops; not to mention the doctor."

"She could be hit by a truck and killed tomorrow."

"We have a perfect case. We have the button he tore off her blazer. We located it in a bar where the rapist drank two drinks and was identified and was seen with it. It connects him to the victim directly."

"So go ahead. You don't need me. Do you want to take it from start to finish?" Scott sounded the least bit edgy. Was this young man overly confident or was this case open and shut?

"Sure, and I've got to see Patricia Rankin."

"See who?" Scott had heard him. He just didn't believe what he'd heard.

"The TV girl on Group One News."

"Why should you?"

"She called us and asked to speak to any DA handling any rape case in this city. They switched her over to me."

Scott didn't say anything for a moment, then: "The victim has a right to privacy. Don't blow the case you are so certain of winning. Why get mixed up with her? She's dynamite."

Fred smiled. "I'll protect the victim's rights, don't worry. I'll also bring a few facts home to Rankin, if she intends to make a mockery of what we're trying to do down here."

"She's smart. I heard her broadcast last Monday. Or was it the Monday before? I know she's gung ho on the subject. So be very careful. Of course, you can ask to be shifted off the case."

Fred stood up. "Are you kidding? This is the most exciting thing that's happened to me since I went down the expert ski hill by mistake. I'm about to set up an appointment with her. Would you like to join us?"

Scott held up his hand. "Not me!" He feigned fear. "She's a lot to handle. Keep me posted and don't let her trap you. Nothing on the air which I haven't okayed, hear?"

"I consider that an order." Fred left.

In the hallway, Fred wondered two things: Why D. P. Scott wore a bow tie? Second: Why the old boy had been so agreeable to him at first sight?

Guy Masters had a lot of time to think in jail. Time to blame what happened on other people . . . society, that girl. First he could fix responsibility on his older brother, Henry. He hadn't shown him the way. Henry had been a copout. And take his father! He had made a big mistake by divorcing Guy's beautiful mother.

His father's first name was Sherwood. His grandparents had named him that after the playwright and poet, Sherwood Anderson, who died in 1931 but was alive when he, Guy's father, was born. Guy's grandparents used to quote, "Everyone in the world is Christ and they are all crucified," from *The Philoso-*

64

pher by Anderson. But Guy couldn't reconcile that with the Bible, nor could his brother. "They gotta be atheists," said Henry wisely when he first heard it at dinner. "There is only one man named Christ and how can we all be Him?"

His father was fat, had no muscle to speak of, and couldn't change a tire. He couldn't even paint a fence without getting paint all over himself, and he didn't like baseball. One day in Springfield, Massachusetts, where his father worked as an accountant, they all went on a picnic, just men and boys. When they got in the woods back of the swimming hole, which had leeches in it, all the kids started stripping and running wild in the woods screaming they were Tarzan. Then the fathers took up the game, taking off their pants yelling, "Where is Jane?" and "Me, Tarzan! Where's Jane?" falling down in a heap on the pine needles under the big trees and laughing themselves sick. But not Guy's father, Sherwood. He wouldn't take his clothes off in front of the men.

So he never could talk to his father about anything, especially about being a man. What would his father know about that? What would he know about sex? Like masturbation. Henry hadn't been very clear to Guy about that as the years went by. You could blame Henry as well as his father for that, too.

"It's gonna fall off if you don't leave it alone!" his brother had said, advising him, too, that you get callouses on your palm. "And then everyone will know what you've been doin."

"Also," his brother had whispered to him one night when they were with another friend in a tree house, "you can go slowly deaf, after a while you can't hear."

"What did you say? I didn't hear you," asked Guy and they all laughed, but it wasn't very funny thinking you would go deaf and insane, too.

A real father could have set him straight. A real father could have done a lot of things.

One day he came home from school back to Longmeadow on the old trolley car tracks, trying to balance on the track and then not walk on a crack in the cement walk because you'd die. Right there! "There was a guy who did that," his brother had once told him. "Was walking along this very cement sidewalk and hit a crack with the toe of his shoe. And splang! Dropped dead of a mysterious jungle disease. They never found out why. But I know. He should not have walked on a crack."

It was like cemeteries. You never walked by or drove by one breathing. If you did, there would be five minutes taken off your life. If you held your breath, you gained three minutes more. That's what everybody knew. In a way Guy still believed it, only now he couldn't figure out if his score was even or he was ahead. Anyway, if they convicted him of this rape, it wouldn't matter.

His father could've helped him out a long time ago, like the time Henry spent the night with Paul and he and his father were home alone.

"Son," said his father, "I wish we were closer. Is there anything that worries you?"

"Yes," Guy had said, putting down his fork. "I am afraid I am insane."

His father's pudgy face dropped and he stared at Guy, as if he were insane. "Why?" he asked.

"I think because I have been memorizing license plates walking home from school."

"Memorizing license plates? What in heaven's name for?"

"That's just it. I don't know. I see an Idaho plate and I memorize it. A Michigan plate I saw today, 067 dash 456, that was an easy one. I guess maybe I think I'll see it again, sometime. I forget them after a while. Then I have to memorize others to keep it up. Am I insane?"

His father had picked up his fork, asked the housekeeper to bring some more potatoes and then, when she had gone, he said, "Never do that again. It means you have a fixation."

"What's that mean?" Guy had asked.

"It's an unhealthy preoccupation with something—like an obsession. You are obsessed. It isn't exactly insane." Then he had started eating again.

"Not exactly?" Guy had asked. "But how close am I? I mean. . . ."

His father had laughed, put down his fork and knife, and eyed him carefully. "Your brother putting crazy ideas in your head, son? He has a weird sense of humor."

"Like what?" Guy was being protective. No point in getting Henry in trouble over license plate memorizing. It had been his own idea. Or fixation.

"About insanity? About . . . er, girls?"

"Girls, yes, Father. Insanity, no. Only about jerkin' off."

That was the end of that heart-to-heart talk. His father had blushed and the housekeeper had come in to clear off the plates. His father just sat there, watching her and shaking his head.

Today Guy had no misleading brother to frighten him—no helpless father to be ashamed of—but he did have a mother (God bless her!) who had hired the tall man standing next to him before the judge.

A thin, sandy-haired fellow with a few freckles

67

stood on the other side of Sturdevant Warren and said he was the assistant district attorney assigned to the case and that his full name was Frederick Osborne Michaels.

Warren, on his behalf, had just made a motion to reduce his bail.

"In view of his confession, I cannot."

Guy shuffled and tried to stand straight and not tremble. It looked serious.

"There are substantial reasons, Your Honor. My client must help support his mother." Masters gulped. Why it was an out-and-out lie! It was she who had supplied him legal fees and the bond money. "She is destitute," he went on, "just enough to be buried. My client, Your Honor, has always supported himself—a wage earner, Your Honor. A substantial man with a background of solid employment. He never lost a day's work. Even now, while he's here, his mother has been depending on him.

"He's a stranger to New York, sir, looking for employment. She may end up on the street! He is no loafer! He attends church!" It was such a clincher, something not to be refuted, to end the matter straight away. Warren turned at the word *church* and looked into Masters's eyes as if in admiration for such a holy, spiritual man.

"Mr. Warren," the judge began after a deep sigh, "I am indeed sorry about his destitute mother's condition, overwhelmed with your recital of his legendary employment record but, as to his remarkable feat of church attendance along with eighty million or so other Americans each Sunday, may I point out to you, a religious scholar, that more crimes of murder and mayhem have been committed in the name of 'religion' than any other on the face of the globe. I give you the Crusades, for example. The fact that a man goes to church may also only mean that he goes there to confess his sins. But it is before a court of law a man must be judged, not merely by God's laws alone. Here it is, one may still hope, that the Judeo-Christian moral codes based on the Ten Commandments and the laws of Moses will be enforced with due justice. As to a point made that your client has never been arrested, has no prior record, and therefore his bail should be lowered, I think you have a point."

"Your Honor," objected Michaels, "this man is a confessed rapist. He must not be allowed to go free on the streets of this city. Not until this case is settled. He is a menace to society and Miss Landress must not be subjected to fear of another attack."

"Your argument is touching," interrupted Warren, "in light of the increased budgets for a larger police force, the formation of crime commissions to stop murder and robbery here. But this young man is no hardened criminal. Right now he must stay in a jail which is notorious for its riots; where conditions lead to violence; where a young, clean-living man like Guy Masters may even be forced into homosexuality!

"This man has no prior record. Not even for a speeding ticket. Look at the yellow sheets! And as for that confession, we'll see about that shortly." Masters felt proud of his lawyer. It was no surprise that his motion to reduce bail was finally granted. The formalities over with, cash bail was immediately supplied and in ten minutes the group, including Michaels, found themselves together in the hall.

Fred was impressed by the older man's performance, recognizing a pro. He turned to Warren, as was the custom between adversaries, and said, "So the great Sturdevant Warren is now into rape. It should help revise the laws in favor of the victims." He smiled, but Warren did not.

"Rape, in itself, is a study. I am interested in the motives, the motivations. I tend to believe the man rather than the woman," replied Warren. "Does it ever occur to us to ponder why indeed a man does commit rape? I apply rationale to law. I recall Oliver Wendell Holmes stating, 'The standards of law are standards of general application. The law,' he said, 'takes no account of the infinite varieties of temperament, intellect, and education which makes the internal characters of a given act'—rape for example— 'so different in different men. It (the law) does not attempt to see them as God sees them, for more than one sufficient reason.'"

"Don't try to relate Holmes's discussions of law to an act of rape," Fred started.

"He also stated that 'the character of every act,' may I remind you, 'depends upon the circumstances in which it is done.'"

"He was speaking of free speech, stating it did not give a man a right to yell 'fire!' in a crowded theatre to cause a panic. Rape is a sexual crime compelling a woman to submit to an intimate act."

"I deplore rape. But in view of promiscuity, how is it intimate?"

"To most of us sex is a private act resulting from mutual love. It is the final consuming act of real love. It cannot be equated with or allied to street crimes. Rape is an act of physical assault upon another person. Your client. . ."

"Is innocent of it."

"We'll see whether the grand jury agrees!" Michaels walked away. Masters stamped out his cigarette and asked, "What in hell was all that about?"

"We're just two war horses snorting. Of course they'll agree. They rubber stamp everything."

Later, Warren did what he had known he would do to start putting things off. He made a motion to examine the evidence and confession in the hands of the DA and asked for a list of the names of witnesses which the DA intended to call. He also asked for a "Huntley Hearing." He could then directly challenge and possibly strike the confession.

Masters wanted to know why the delay. "Can't you hurry this up?"

"Lawyers learn to be masters of delay. The longer he puts it off, the more chance his opponent will tire, will give up. Someone involved with the case may die, or move away. He wants his opposition to lose steam. Keep cool! Get a job. Do something. But wait. Time is on our side."

Six

The man in workman's clothing had difficulty reading the names of the people living in the small apartment house.

"Why the hell doesn't someone take the trouble to type out nameplates? Every one of these is unreadable." Then he found TREADWELL-LANDRESS, in Susan's best penmanship.

Working as "Sturdy" Warren's investigator had paid off over the years. Lately old Sturdy had been cooling it, but a criminal attorney needed private investigators. Warren had called him. "Plant a bug at this address. Do it without letting anyone know you got in or out. Get me tapes."

He had choices. "A telephone tap?" "No good!" Sturdy said. "I want what goes on in bed."

The man started hitting bells, all down the line. Someone would be in, someone stupid enough to let him in.

Sure enough, after a moment, a voice over the intercom asked, "Who is it?"

"Telephone man."

"My phone's okay."

"It's your line, lady, shorting out the whole building."

The buzzer sounded and the locks clicked open. He was in!

He wore a blue denim shirt, blue pants, and a large black belt about his waist from which hung the tools of a telephone repairman. He would walk to the second floor, listen at the door, make certain no one was in, and plant the bug. If anyone was there, he'd beat a retreat and come back after surveillance proved it was empty.

He stood at her door, but suddenly he heard someone coming toward it. He moved quickly to face the elevator door and pushed the "down" button. A woman brushed into him and stood at the elevator door.

"Oops! I'm sorry," she said in a pleasant voice. He hoped this wasn't the girl. She was cute and blonde. He let her have his sincere look. "I'm checking out the building for Ma Bell. You go ahead."

She must be going shopping, he thought. She carried one of those empty knit bags. He'd have to hurry. Ten keys later and he was inside the apartment.

Twenty minutes later it was thoroughly bugged. Particularly the beds. No one could turn in bed without the earphones in the basement getting the message. Down in the basement he rented a small room for thirty days. "I have to be where nothing disturbs me," he had said to the grateful landlord. "I am taking a medical exam."

He would leave the tape machine on. Whenever someone came into the apartment on the second floor, the switch would activate and the tape would record every word. He would be back at eight each night.

He would soon be delivering a record of events as they took place in the beds of the Treadwell-Landress apartment.

He stationed himself and waited. A small window looking up at the steps leading into the apartment house permitted him to watch who went in and who came out. The noise made by the elevator motor revealed when it was running. He soon had logged the run time to each floor.

Susan returned several hours later, and shortly afterwards Anne arrived with a friend. The tapes whirled on, recording a perfectly normal conversation between three girls. "Hi, Susan, this is Beatrix. She's a friend from the airlines, just in for a few days."

"Nice to meet you. You know, I was planning on going to a movie tonight. There's a Tracy-Hepburn flick playing up the street at that revival house. Wouldn't you two like to come along?"

"No ... we have a lot of catching up to do ... it's been a long time. . . .Come on in the kitchen, Beatrix. I'll fix you a drink."

The voices faded away, and shortly thereafter the door slammed, and the elevator descended from the second floor. He watched the door, and saw one of the girls leave.

Later he heard the story of the last several years of Beatrix's life—her experiments with drugs, her travels and love affairs, and then he was filled in on Anne's life—her job, her family, her love affairs. The

74

conversation was animated and sometimes giddy. The more they drank, the more they talked. After several hours, he heard one of them say, "Hey, you wanna smoke some grass?" and he turned up the volume on his earphones.

"Sure, why not?" After a while he heard some sighs and whispers and "How do you feel?" "Far out." And then, "Come here, come a little closer." And then more whispers and sighs. Then he heard the voices again, this time saying things which shocked him. Old Sturdy Warren was really going to get his money's worth this time.

At his apartment house door, Sturdevant Warren met his investigator with a whiskey glass in hand. It was ten in the morning.

"Up all night, boss?" he asked as he was shown in. The five-room suite was a contrast to that of the girls under observation. Located at 124 East Seventy-fourth, an upper-middle-class neighborhood, it was decorated in muted tones, and though it was elegant it was also coldly severe.

He was led into a den with a TV, walnut paneling, and a large leather sofa. It was the only lived-in room in an otherwise sterile-appearing apartment.

"I drink in the morning—one shot—it fixes me up for the day. Starts the old heart." The white-haired man with the ruddy face tapped his chest and smiled with all his teeth showing. "What have you got for me?"

The investigator placed two half-hour tapes on top of his walnut desk and said, "A bombshell."

"If it is, I'll double what I said you'd get. If it isn't, you'll try again. Now, you beat it. I have work to do."

He took the envelope Warren offered him, walked

quickly to the door. "You better put your player on high. The volume is very low on that tape. The girls weren't exactly yelling."

Ten minutes later Sturdevant Warren had heard the tapes and was getting dressed. What he had heard had startled him. He knew that it would startle a judge and jury, too.

"That dirty woman . . ." he kept saying. "That filthy slut!"

At Sixty-second and Second Warren got out of his taxi, surveyed the area, and headed toward the brownstone. On the second floor, he rang the bell. Michael Rose's secretary came to the door.

"Can I help you?"

"I want to see Mr. Rose. I have no appointment, but if he is in, tell him it is most urgent. I am an attorney representing a client."

He had chosen and rehearsed his opening line. They would, of course, being in advertising, presume that he meant one of their clients.

The door opened wide and he was shown into a small room. Behind a desk sat a fat balding man with squinted eyes and a pale complexion.

"Mr. Rose, this is Sturdevant Warren. He is an attorney and represents a client." Rose got up immediately and stuck out a hand. Warren smiled, took the hand, dropped it, sat down, lit a cigar, and let Rose watch him look over the pictures of models on Rose's desk. Some of them were in bikinis, some in the nude.

"You have a pleasant job, sir . . ." he started.

"Do you want Miss Carena to bring you some coffee?"

"No, thank you." The dark-haired girl left quietly and closed the door behind her at a wave of Rose's hand.

76

"I do have a pleasant job . . . and I love my work."
Rose's smile froze and he seemed to be wondering
what this distinguished looking man was up to in his
office this morning.

"We have heard of an employee of yours named
. . ." Warren took an envelope from his pocket and
looked at some scribbling on the back of it. ". . . Name
of Susan Chont Landress. May I see her?"

Rose was startled. He shifted nervously and
watching Warren's cigar smoke, lit his own. The
bastard had two more and hadn't offered him one.
Must be a stingy son of a bitch. "No. I am sorry, but
we let her go."

"Ah . . . aaaah! I see. You found out."

"Found out? What do you mean?" Rose felt the
blood in his cheeks.

"About her . . . you, too. Then I don't have to tell you
that my client would be deeply upset had you any
pictures in your file intended to be used in ads for
which she had posed. In fact . . ." he paused . . . "my
client would pay well for any prints or negatives of
shots of her just to be certain no pictures of her were
ever used. You see, we don't want to happen to us
what happened to that big soap company and that girl
who appeared in X-rated films . . ." He let it hang
there, waiting.

He didn't have long. Rose must have pushed a
hidden buzzer, for Miss Carena was in the door. "Joe-
Ann," he said. "I mean, Miss Carena, please bring
me the entire picture file on Susan Landress—the girl
I had to fire."

With the large envelope between his knees, Warren
sat in the taxi on his way to his office. He had just
glanced at the twelve or so enlargements which
would be very interesting to the judge and jury.

No wonder, he thought after looking at them, that his poor client Guy Masters had been enticed by that girl! Good God, an angel would have succumbed!

It was six again and the stool on which Patricia sat was twirled higher, until her eyes were on level with the camera lens.

She set her smile and waited.

Voiceover: "And tonight Patricia Rankin picks up where she left off last Monday night on the grim story of rape. Tonight her subject is 'The Relationship.'"

She began: "We commonly think of rape as a crime committed by a stranger. An unknown psychopath who creeps out of the shadows and attacks an innocent passerby.

"While this is sometimes the case, the opposite is equally true. If you are raped, the chances are about fifty-fifty that you'll know the man who rapes you. Sound incredible? The National Commission on the Causes of Violence recently found that in twenty-nine percent of the recorded rapes the rapist and his victim were acquaintances, and that ten percent of the rapes occurred between members of the same family.

"And a recent study in Philadelphia, reported in *Sexual Behavior* magazine, showed that thirty-four percent of the cases involved people who were friends, acquaintances, or neighbors. In fourteen percent of the cases, the rapists and victims were even closer friends or relatives.

"What does this mean to a woman? That every man she knows is a potential rapist? No. But the fact that so many rapists and victims know each other presents special problems in court. The existence of a relationship between the man and the woman before the rape may cast doubt on the victim's testimony.

The police and courts will suspect that sometime previous to the rape, the victim led the rapist to believe that they were going to have sex together. As you know, the male-oriented legal system is always ready to believe that rape is actually the woman's fault. In fact, the first question the police often ask is, 'Did you know him?' And if the answer is 'yes,' the chances are good that they will refuse to investigate the case.

"What can a woman do to prevent this kind of rape in the first place? Rape by someone she knows? Not much, but there are a few things to keep in mind.

"All young girls should be told at an early age about 'funny uncles,' men who may not be uncles at all, but simply neighbors or friends of the family. Girls should be warned early, and reminded occasionally, that if a man, or an older boy, embarrasses them or makes them feel uncomfortable, acts 'funny' with them, they should get away from him immediately and tell a grownup.

"In regard to neighbors, family friends, acquaintances and relatives, women can only be aware of the possibility, and be careful not to parade in front of open windows or unwittingly entice in any way.

"One further caution about rape by someone you know—a caution especially to you young women who frequent the singles bars and feel perfectly at ease picking up a new friend. More than one young woman has casually left a bar to go to a man's apartment or her own 'for dinner,' 'to look at my seashell collection,' or 'to pick up a warmer jacket' and has been raped. And what can she say to the police? She went willingly to his apartment or invited him into hers, and she's going to have a hard time proving in court that she had no idea what was going to happen.

"In addition, there is a relationship between

drinking and rape. Drinking relationships between strangers can become highly emotional, with both the man and the woman seeking an intense or intimate relationship. The caution is simply to know what you want, how far you intend to go, and to immediately reject, in a strong way, any advances you are not interested in. I don't mean to sound like an old mother hen; we must be aware of these possibilities. Our lives depend on it.

"More on rape next Monday—where rapes occur, and how to fight. This is Patricia Rankin for Group One News."

"This is Group One News saying. . ."

Patricia was worn out. But she pulled herself together for the meeting. A man from the district attorney's office was sitting in the reception room waiting for her. Once in her room, and with some of the makeup off, she asked them to send him in.

He stood in the doorway for a moment, unsure whether this attractive woman actually meant for him to come in. She was sitting with her head in her hands at a desk overflowing with papers, books, ashtrays, and convenience food wrappers. She looked totally exhausted. He wondered if she had been crying.

"I'm Fred Michaels," he said. "I'm so glad to meet you. I have admired. . ."

She looked up and waved him to the big leather chair, her only concession to visitors, usually reserved for Joe. "Please, Fred, sit down. Would you care for a drink?"

He said yes. She poured a Scotch for them both, while they sized one another up.

"You were a lawyer before you joined the DA's staff?" she started.

"Yes. I worked up in the Bronx. Small firm. Handling crime. Had a slew of clients. Came to old D.P.'s attention. He's the city's rape expert, you might say. I'm a Fordham alumnus. Live downtown near the office ... view up and down the river." He lit two cigarettes, passed her one. "And you...? Did you broadcast before this?" He waved his hand about. She noticed the long fingers. His shoes were well polished, nails clean, hair neat, white shirt and dark blue tie. He wore flared pants and a wide lapeled suit. He smiled.

"For ten years in Minneapolis, then here as a producer's assistant. I got into setting up women's shows and they handed me this number to do on the air. Well, it worked."

"It certainly did!"

"You know why I called your office. I liked Scott. He called me back ... and warned me not to go too far."

"And set this date. Nice guy. Could have made it at nine in the morning. I watched your show from the reception room. You're good. I'm as interested in the woman's side as I guess you are ... almost. I have some ideas about it."

"Want to tell me?"

"Not really ... at least until my ideas are formulated." He stamped out the cigarette and leaned back. She knew the symptoms. He'd start talking if she encouraged him.

"It's about damages."

"Damages? For whom?"

"You women. You get raped, okay? And you run to us ... criminal case. . . . Then we put a guy away ... maybe. . . .But what do you get out of it?"

"Revenge. Seeing the guy get it ... so no other woman will be his victim."

"Nuts! You get nothing. Except the humiliation of police, hospital, court procedures, and the public disgrace. Many raped women are later divorced. Their husbands somehow blame them. They don't want a soiled body. You know what I mean. Women move away—change their names—can't forget the scene—take to drugs or booze or. . ."

"Okay, so what's your damage bit? How would that work?"

"Well, I'm a lawyer and you're a woman's-angle TV broadcaster and I respect your profession. So you respect mine, okay?"

She nodded and sipped her Scotch.

"Make rape both a civil and criminal offense at the same time, with evidence interlocking so that the DA's office doing the work for the people can also be doing the work for the girl, the individual victim. Today if she 'wins' a rape case in the criminal court she can collect no damages. In my scheme, after conviction the jury would be sent out again to fix the money damages. The cost, of course, is what stops most people from suing in civil courts. A woman who was raped might be able to collect damages as if she had been assaulted or hit by a car or struck by a falling object, and so forth."

"The problem is that rapists are usually poor. How could they pay a judgment?"

Fred acknowledged the problem with a nod, and Patricia continued, "I thought in criminal cases the People had to come in with evidence of guilt beyond any reasonable doubt. Would that be necessary in a civil rape case?" She leaned forward. Fred's voice was pleasant. She could see him before a judge. Tall, a bit gaunt, but with those expressive hands!

"No ... it would not! Now rape bail is being increased to $25,000 as a deterrent and they have taken away the need for total corroboration and the law people upstate are doing a lot for the women ... bail to deter the man, no corroboration of the various factors which constitute Rape One, Two, or Three, to help the woman in court, but still no recompense for her trouble ... her pain and anguish. All one gets is a civil case against a deadbeat!"

"Damages for rape? I'll think about that. Try it out. But tell me, Fred, how did you get into this subject so deeply? Normally men laugh at rape. It's the subject of locker room jokes. It's a gag. Women don't get raped. They ask for it. You know what I mean?"

"I heard about the judge once who held up an inkwell, gave the victim's lawyer a pen, and said, 'Go ahead. Put the pen in that hole.' Then he started moving the inkwell around. It's an old story. They call it 'the moving target' theory in the law school dorms. Of course a woman can't be an inkwell, not when she's gang-raped or the guy has a gun at her head. But it's a part of the male legend that women like it, finally succumb to the dominant male. There's even a part in the judge's charge to a rape jury where he points out the law which states that if she stopped fighting back and let him proceed, she hasn't been raped!"

"So you took the woman's side."

"There is no one side. Take me. I'm a man or consider myself one. And when I was a kid, my mother dominated me, and my sister was a tiger—strong-willed. So I suppose according to the charts you use—I'm a potential rapist, having been dominated by women. Wrong! The female superiority bit never bugged me. An overly domineering woman doesn't appeal to me, sexually, but she isn't . . . a woman!"

"You're a rapist at heart, but you control it?"

"I know you're baiting me. It shows me you're interested in me or my subject! But actually, no. I take out my aggressions in my power struggle against women by loving them for what they are—equals. If I respect myself, I have to respect them. If the available woman is around for a rapist, he'll take out or express that fear in a flash. I understand that a lot of rapists are afraid to have sex with a mature woman because they feel inadequate; they fear they can't perform. They seek out prostitutes."

"Thanks for reminding me. I almost forgot that point." He wasn't sure if she was being sarcastic, but he had no idea of stopping. "Prostitutes would permit sadism or masochism. So the rapist gets 'his thing.' In countries where prostitution is legal, there is less rape." She made another note.

"Where do I get background on that point?"

"I have some books. I'll loan them to you. After dinner I'll go get 'em."

"After what dinner?"

"Like . . . now?" He stood up, his brows crinkling.

"I thought you'd never ask."

Seven

The first meeting between Fred and Susan had gone
well. He had arranged for her to come to his office at
100 Centre Street when no one else was there. She
acted as if she trusted him and he responded to her
questions in detail. "I like a dentist who tells me it's
going to hurt," he had said. "Then I can get prepared
for it. Well, Miss Landress, this is going to hurt. Are
you certain you wish to endure the proceedings, the
jury picking, the trial?"

"Yes."

"Do you really know what lies ahead?"

"I think so. I've got to go through a lot of questioning."

"From now on most of it will come from Masters's
lawyer. He will villify you, try to trap you, try to prove
that you enticed his client."

"You've got to be kidding!"

"It's his only defense. He'll pry into your background. He'll try to get you to admit you were playing

around, that you dated strange men, and that you were and are 'a loose woman.' The jurors will hear all this. When you get a group of twelve people together making a decision relative to morals, they tend to be over-prudish."

"I can't understand that, but I. . . ." She seemed to hesitate. "I don't know why I should be subjected to this. He raped me. The thing I don't understand is why anyone in the jury should care about my background. How about his!"

"Inadmissible. Even if he was charged with rape a hundred times before. Only prior convictions can be introduced *if the defendant takes the stand.* It's considered prejudicial. Your past—okay. His—no dice."

"They say, 'Lay back and enjoy it.' I guess that's what I should have done."

"Yes, I've heard that bit of advice, but it's false. It's as antiquated as the law I work under. Forty percent of the rapes are combined with brutality—a high percentage involve gang rape—and I doubt any girl could enjoy that! In fact the joke—which is what it is after all—could have only been based on the lore that women enjoy rape in the first place!"

"You sound like someone who's done a lot of thinking about rape."

"Haven't you? Most women do, don't they?"

Susan wrinkled her brow, played with a letter opener on his small green steel desk, looked out to the wall outside his window. "Nope. Not before this."

"Well, from now on you'll be hearing, breathing, feeling, sensing, thinking, and speaking about nothing else. Don't back out during the trial.

Warren, the lawyer who's taken Masters's case, is a wise old fox, a man who will stoop to anything to get his man off—mainly because it's his first rape case, even though he has practiced criminal law for a generation before the same judges."

"And I'll be crucified?"

"Expect to be. He'll try to get you to disappear, to evaporate. Your witnesses as well. The defense attorney will bear down so hard on them they'll say, 'Well, I don't really remember' or 'Come to think of it, it wasn't that definite' and so forth—once the whole thing is underway and the DA has been counting on you and the witnesses."

"You mean Julia McElroy?"

"Yes, and Joe Cartona and the cops . . . and the doctor."

"You can count on Mrs. McElroy. She's a good woman. But who is that other person?"

"Joe Cartona is the bartender who saw Masters right after the ra. . .the attack upon you."

"Go ahead and say it—r-a-p-e, rape!"

". . . .I know. It's a hell of a word. I want you to be strong. Do you think you can be?"

"I'll answer questions. I won't break down and cry. I just don't want my mother, and Dougie, my brother, to ever ever hear about it."

"They might."

"Can't I use another name?"

"No, you can't. You are only a complainant. It's the 'People against Guy Masters.' It's criminal to rape. He can get twenty-five years. He is up on a serious charge. In some states death sentences are mandatory."

"He should be hanged by the neck until he is dead—in the marketplace."

"You sound like a European."

She smiled in a way that told him she was proud of

her answer. "I am Belgian—a couple of generations back. In fact my father's parents came from the city of Ghent."

"I've asked permission of my boss if you can be interviewed by a top TV personality. Not on the air, of course. That would cause a mistrial. You'll remain anonymous. You'll be protected. She's doing a series on rape and wants to get some attitudes from a victim —the woman's side. Would you agree to this? You don't have to."

"What kind of a woman is she? She must be morbid."

"Not morbid . . . curious. She's done some pretty heavy things about women and drugs. I hope she'll throw a spotlight on what's happening in this city. There's been a lot of stuff in the papers about our Rape Squad and the outsiders are now looking in. The fact a top TV newscaster is about to do a series on rape on a national basis should spark some further improvement in the conditions which women face."

"A woman's liberationist?"

"No. Not exactly . . . but keen on women's rights . . . all that. She's also a very nice person."

"What could I do? I mean . . . after all, I don't want this to be dragged out in public. I'm upset enough as it is."

"Nothing public. In fact, though she had hoped to put you on, neither Scott nor the department will allow it. Not someone in court and a supposed rape victim. May blow the case."

"I answer questions?"

"As best you can. Get your point across."

"What point, Mr. Michaels? I'm not selling anyone anything."

"You're a wronged woman facing a situation which is nearly hopeless. If it weren't for that confession and a few tangible bits of material evidence and a good witness . . . he'd get off and go away smiling."

She didn't respond; just gritted her teeth. "I hate him! I'll see her."

He set up a date for the two women to meet in the Palm Court of the Plaza Hotel. There, the dignified atmosphere, the palms, high ceiling, the elegant ladies and their escorts, all provided a discreet atmosphere and helped overcome Susan's original shyness at meeting such a well-known woman.

They started with consomme and had a chicken salad, discussing backgrounds, their families, the hassle of being free and female in a big city.

Susan immediately liked the petite and enthusiastic woman, just a few years her senior. Her face was in constant motion, eyebrows mobile and eyes concerned as she listened.

"I wanted to get your gut reaction. I can't put you on the air, though victims have been interviewed on radio and TV after the court case is over. I want this to be understated. Not a sensational exposé kind of thing, as if mankind had just discovered rape was going on. I believe this total national concern is a bit tardy. Women have been aware of the growing threat —the increase in incidence, if you'll allow the trite way of stating it—for years and years. Now, suddenly, it's become commercial. On the air, in magazines. Freelance writers are making coin out of female attitudes—well, Miss Landress, mine will be a study and I hope interesting enough to make people think! You can't say much on the air because of the time commitment, nor in a TV feature either. In effect, I want every second to lead the viewer along to a conclusion in the end."

"To think about what . . . in the end?" Susan had

worn a suit, and pinned her hair up. She felt very chic and very much a part of New York, sitting at lunch with another attractive young woman. She sensed something righteous in the situation, that Patricia was interested in something bigger than just what had happened to her.

"To write letters to congressmen and state officials ... to put a bite into the law—perhaps to discover a way in which a raped woman could recover damages."

Susan waited. She had thought of that, but in a different way. Sure, a woman had been victimized, had been hurt. But what good was it going to the police, enduring all the interrogation if nothing came of it—for her?

"I need your honest answer. For example, your emotional reaction," she prodded after they had finished their lunch. "Can you tell me what you were thinking when you went into that park and how you felt later? I mean you were practically carried out, weren't you?"

"I was. The first thing I remember was this woman's voice. I couldn't believe what had happened to me. I went in that park completely unaware of what might happen. Oh, I read about this city. It's known all over the country that it's not too safe in Central Park, but who would expect to be attacked right on the sidewalk, twenty feet away from huge apartment houses with doormen?"

"We heard a story from Los Angeles out where you lived, where a rather elderly woman was raped in full view of men and passing women in a parking lot ... in broad daylight. There are many such cases, I guess. How did you feel when you heard the woman's voice?"

"Like she was an angel! I was beaten, bruised, and hurt all over. I froze at some point and shut it . . . shut it all off. I felt like I was being ground up and tossed into a garbage truck. The guy I saw at the police round-up. . ."

"Lineup."

". . . .lineup. It was him, alright. If I had had my brother here, well, he would have killed him. Hanging isn't good enough. Do you know how disgusted and ashamed I feel?"

The waiter looked at her, paused, and placed the dish in front of her. Susan realized she must have raised her voice.

"Go on . . . about the hospital. . . ."

"It was degrading. No privacy. But they have so many people waiting. I felt like a sheep in one of those slaughterhouses—'You're next. Slice! You're next! Snip!' Humiliating isn't the word. Then the police. They acted as if I was a prostitute. I think they held back because an older woman, Mrs. McElroy, was there. I had the feeling that usually rape victims are choice entertainment down there. That they really love going over the juicy details."

"I'll cover the insensitive treatment, a woman's need for a woman's ear with the police, the district attorney, and the inevitable accusation that the victim actually led the rapist on."

"Aren't there women you can talk to at some police departments? It would be a lot easier to tell a woman about it."

"They are available. But now you have to put yourself totally in the hands of your DA. The only way to put the man behind bars is to prepare yourself for the worst. They'll try to 'impeach' your morality. They'll ask about your childhood, Michaels tells me.

Did you date? With whom? As if you were a sex freak. Not one vulnerable point could be overlooked—even a divorce."

"Divorce? Are you kidding? Why one out of every three. . ."

"A divorced woman, in the male eye, is fair game. She's had affairs and she wants more, now that her husband and she are separated. It figures."

"Men are stupid."

"Let's tell them so and try to straighten out a few of their kinks. You lived with an invalid mother. Your brother is a Viet Nam hero. With ribbons. It helps."

"I never thought of him or his ribbons in that capacity before. It's lucky they don't check out my father. He's a dropout, but lovable, and has a tendency to disappear."

"Just another reason to feel that men don't always know what in hell is really happening on this uptight little planet!"

After dropping Susan off at her apartment, Patricia decided to begin a background survey of her particular case. She directed the taxi to drop her off at the park where Susan had been attacked. She walked down the circular path to where Susan had told her the man had come upon her. Then she studied the distances to the East River, to the doorways of apartments and the sidewalk to the street, becoming aware from a personal standpoint how near civilization must have been to the "jungle kill."

Patricia had discussed rape with many psychiatrists and several medical men. They all agreed that the force used upon a victim, though sudden, did not render them insensitive to the abuse during the crime. "Those who submitted and did so only because a knife was thrust at their throat must suffer a great deal more emotional after-shock than those who had been knocked down, beaten, and endured the attack nearly or completely unconscious of what was happening to them."

She had earlier decided to stay far away from the psychological trauma of rape in her broadcasts, since she would be treading on dangerous ground, but she did not agree with Joe Fontana that she shouldn't put a psychiatrist on in person.

In the case of a rapist, she had been told by a leading forensic doctor, "We often suggest mental treatment. In fact, in some states it is mandatory before his trial or after it before he starts serving his sentence, if convicted." That had been in Connecticut.

But Patricia Rankin's concerns were not totally with the rapist or the victim. She decided to make a trip north at her earliest convenience to look into the past of Susan's attacker, Guy Masters, to see what that past might have contributed to the present. From Susan and their two-hour luncheon and trip in the cab, she could see that the girl, raised in the sun on the beach of a California city, was completely innocent, had not enticed the man, had simply been doing what seemed perfectly natural for her to do— taking a walk outdoors to collect her thoughts. Then, apparently, after the nightmare of the rape, the investigation, and the horror of repeating details, she had had an unhappy three weeks on a rather peculiar job.

"It must have been like a kind of second rape," she had observed. From the startled look on the girl's face, she knew that that was just what it had been.

Eight

In her studio apartment, Susan listened to Patricia finish her broadcast on the setting for rape.

"Remember nearly twenty percent of those rapes occurred in cars. Hitchhiking may be the most expensive ride you ever take."

The announcer concluded Patricia's broadcast with a promise that next Monday's review would cover a specific case.

Susan leaned back, shut out the light, and snapped off the TV.

She had grown accustomed to the opening and closing of the small elevator as it discharged and took on passengers in the small hallway in front of her apartment. It had become an unconscious presence, a kind of humming as it rose and fell, with the clanging of the door at her floor happening at distant intervals.

At 1:00 A.M., though, the humming noise, the grinding and slamming, was unusual. It awakened

94

her and she lay listening, sprawled across the large sofa bed open in the main room, the window of the second floor apartment open to the street.

Someone stepped off the elevator onto her floor. She tensed listening, waiting for them to go wherever they were going. But whoever it was didn't move. The footsteps would be loud and clear on the cement floor. No one moved out there. Who was it and what was he doing? What was he waiting for?

Why did she think it was a he?

Quietly, Susan rose, and started toward the door. Perhaps it was Anne, fumbling for her key, home late; or a guest of that guy who lived in the back apartment. She tiptoed toward her door. It was made of steel and had three locks. One turned by a switch lever. The other required a Medico key. The last was the chain. She felt uncomfortable nonetheless.

Maybe she was getting paranoid with all this. When would it end?

She looked through the tiny peep hole.

An eye!

An oval, huge, brown eye stared straight back at her, then he pulled back and she could see his brows were heavy and black!

She screamed. It came instinctively and loud. She started to shake, and toss her head about, trying to get rid of the sight. His predatory, leering face!

He *was* out there!

Bent on getting in, beating her, humiliating and hurting her—again and again!

Susan sank to the floor sobbing, hysterical.

When she calmed down, she was covered with perspiration, and her mouth sagged. She crouched in a corner and stared wildly about her, panting like a trapped animal. Then she rose, holding on to the doorknob, finding her feet with great effort, and stumbled to the bathroom and lowered herself over the toilet bowl head first and retched.

At eight the next morning, she awoke laying criss-cross on her bed. The window curtains danced on a northerly wind, the sounds of cars and buses, horns, and the cries of early shoppers aroused her.

She must call the police.

It was 8:03 A.M. when she had dialed 911. Central routed her call to the nearest patrol car. In twenty-two minutes she heard the familiar sound of a siren, then a doorbell being sounded in the super's base-ment apartment, long enough to bring him running from any of the four floors.

She looked out. The Midtown North blue police car with revolving bubbles stood at the curb. Some inter-ested shopkeepers watched the men at the apartment house door.

"Another ripoff?" asked the cigar stand owner.

"Nope. It's nothing serious. Break it up!" Two cops soon stood at her door with their hats in their hands. One had his memo book ready. The other, the man with grey hair, said his name was Levy.

"You called about a break in?"

"It was Masters—Guy Masters, the man who raped me. I know it was!"

"Tell me all about it," said Levy. The other cop looked at his partner significantly and said, "Yeah, lady. I know a guy tried to rape you. Give us a description of the man and tell us how it happened—all of it. Officer Levy will take it all down."

"Yeah, lady, then we'll just hustle you off to the hospital. . ."

Oh, Christ . . . Oh, God. When would it end! What was happening to her? And why her!

"Never mind the hospital! Never mind writing it down! I've had a preliminary hearing and a Grand Jury. I've had enough! Please, thanks ... thanks a lot. Never mind, he's gone." She closed the door on them and they left quickly, obviously glad to be saved the paper work. "Give me Patricia Rankin," she said into the telephone. "Hurry."

"Without your mother—and money—you'd have been in prison all this time," Warren told his client as they approached the large grey stone building at 100 Centre Street in the Wall Street section of Manhattan.

"Yes, Mom came through," answered Masters. He looked completely different. Under instructions from his attorney, he had used some of the money his mother had sent him to buy a white shirt which he wore open at the neck. A dark blue suit normally for Sunday wear had been shipped him from Bridgeport by his old landlady, glad to see the last of "that frightening man." He looked indeed very "square," very docile and, as instructed, made no sudden jerky moves, nor displayed any unseemly emotion. Masters felt on top of his situation, a man of substance, a man with a formidable attorney, and a man whose slight and quick brush with the law would soon be over.

"You look just fine," the distinguished older man advised him with a nod of approval. He stood like a greying warrior, every wrinkle indicating strength gained from winning. He held his narrow shoulders straight, a loose-fitting black silk suit hanging casually upon the old bones which had not lost their bounce.

Truly they looked a victorious team. Warren's last words still rang in the accused rapist's ear, "Address the judge as 'Your Honor' . . . look straight at him . . . no fidgeting, no grimacing, no dozing off. This is your life they are discussing!"

As they took seats, Fred appeared and walked down to the front of the arena. In his hand he carried a large legal briefcase. It was jammed with papers. Warren nudged his client. "That's my opponent. A newcomer. I'll eat him alive."

In a corner, jammed against two men in sweaty shirts, sat a pretty young girl sobbing. Seated behind her, Warren and Fred waited to be given the room number where they were to report for trial. Hundreds of people were jammed into the room, waiting, and the air stank of dirty clothing and perspiration.

"Any second now the judge will come in and we, along with the rest of this mob, will be sent to different parts of this building." One hour later it became obvious to Masters that his was not a head-line case and that no one cared whether his trial was held or not. The judge had made a hasty late entrance to the sudden cry, "All rise!" intoned without em-phasis but somehow implying dire consequences if anyone sat and ignored the command. Names were called out.

"Clarke" yelled the clerk calling the first on the list. "Ronald W. Clarke!" The lawyer for Clarke said his client was sick and handed the judge a medical report.

The assistant district attorney said he was sick, too. "Sick of waiting for Clarke."

The judge quietly allowed Clarke another two weeks.

"Stern!" barked the clerk. "Robert P. Stern!" Stern was in Puerto Rico where he owned a chain of seafood restaurants. His attorney said, "He planned to be here at the last date but now...well, now it's the height of the season there." Stern's case was adjourned. The judge said, "It is the height of the legal season here. Have him here in two weeks or we'll have him here on a bench warrant. This matter is set for a Huntley Hearing today."

"Masters!" the clerk called. "Find seats!"

Another clerk handed the judge a note. Fred had a moment to reflect. Warren had had his brief prelim and had examined Susan. Then she had braved it through a Grand Jury to be stared at by strange but friendly eyes. How would she stand up at the trial?

The judge looked up. "Are the People ready for the Huntley?"

"We have the police officers on telephone notice, Your Honor."

"Marked ready for Huntley in 10 days. No adjournments. Have the officers in court."

Fred knew what he had to do. He went immediately to his office and put in a call to Julia McElroy, his witness, and then to the hospital for the papers proving rape had taken place. After the details had been arranged, he would drop in on Patricia and take her home from the studio.

Susan Landress had not been in court. Fred wanted her out of sight, and not within range of any possible scare tactic. The midnight visitor, possibly Masters himself, was too frightening. After he said good night to Patricia, Fred went home to his studio apartment on Eleventh Street and sat up all night with paper and pen working over his possibilities.

He had set up an appointment with Mrs. McElroy, whom he trusted. She had hinted though that she might be getting married soon. It meant she might not be around for a trial. But she had to be. The papers from the hospital were being brought over to his office. He wanted to make certain they would be available—that the physician wouldn't forget Susan Landress's thorough gynecological examination.

He was ready by six for a shot of coffee. The hearing was called for in ten days. He made it to the office by nine and asked to see Scott.

He spent thirty minutes with the expert and left feeling more secure. "For God's sake, you've got that button from her blouse. It was torn off during the attack and seen in his hands by a reliable witness and we have two cops to substantiate that!"

Scott was right.

He met with Julia and told her to stand by.

"I don't think I'll need you until we pick a jury and I've called other witnesses. You'll be last."

"I hope so," she had said, looking trim and neat across his desk. She had worn a headband of something which looked like leopard skin, a form-fitting leopard coat, and her dark hair had been contrast to her extremely white skin. "I plan to get married again. A man whom I've known for years. He loves my children. I know it'll be best. Tomorrow we are meeting to make final plans. I may go to visit him. . ."

"Where does he live?"

"Switzerland. He's a cell-cure expert. The best."

"I'll call you as soon as possible but not tomorrow."

She stood up, sighed deeply, and kept the grim look. "I've worried so about Susan. I know that if I hadn't helped the poor girl she'd have been ignored by . . . well, so many people just let others die. Right on the street. You never know when a man begs a dime whether it's because he wants to eat or drink whisky. I always give them something. Don't you?" She started for the door, an extremely sensitive and attractive woman.

"Not always," Fred admitted. "I'd like to investigate each of them first."

"In Susan's case, there was no need. Well, goodbye, Mr. Michaels. You're a nice man."

The hearing day came and Fred found himself looking forward to the exchange. He'd sink the old bastard this time. Patricia had promised to report the results of the hearing as favorably to him as she could. "We report news, we don't slant it. But I know you'll come away with a winner today. Will there be people there in court? Is it open to the public?"

"Why not? It's a People versus Masters case—a rape case with a confession. We've got him with the goods. It's my first case and I can't lose—not with old D.P. looking over my shoulder, and besides I'll win it anyway. I'm not afraid. I just want to put that bastard away." Now it was time.

Michaels saw Masters sitting over there looking rather ordinary—certainly not like the bum the cops had described, and his attorney had dressed for the occasion. He saw his witnesses waiting, two cops looking glum and out of place.

He called as his first witness former Officer, now Detective, Paul Bernard.

"Please tell us what happened when you received the order to proceed to First Avenue and Sixty-third Street where a prowler had been reported."

Bernard had an authoritative mien. Politely, he asked, "May I omit some of the routine details and concentrate on the action that now seems pertinent?"

"By all means, Detective Bernard." Fred was

101

pleased with Bernard. What a beautiful voice for the hearing room.

"We saw the man, later identified as Guy Masters, at a door trying to get in."

"You approached him, of course?"

"We approached him and he said he was looking for a men's room. My partner. . ."

"Objection!" Warren shouted. "We'll have his partner on the stand in due time. Witness should confine himself to his personal testimony and counsel should stop leading."

"Sustained," the judge droned.

"I asked him what he was doing."

"And he told you he was seeking a men's room, is that right?"

"Right."

"Then what did you do?"

"I stepped aside. My partner had a few questions." Bernard glanced at Warren. "He can tell you about the line he took."

"Did you suggest to your partner any course of action?"

"In my judgment, the man was bombed, dirty, and suspicious. I suggested he be brought to the precinct. My partner agreed and we brought him in."

"One other question. You searched him there on the scene?"

"Yes sir. Negative. No weapons."

"Did you then advise him of his rights before you took him in?"

"Yes sir. Standard procedure."

"Then you brought him to the precinct house?"

"We were going to charge him with attempted burglary, but at that point, Sergeant Joe Gerlach came forward and said he believed the prisoner answered a general alert out for a man accused of a

Rape One charge. He was then led away for further questioning by other officers."

It was Warren's turn with the witness. He came on, coat open, fingers tucked into his back belt loops.

"You've had a promotion, haven't you?"

"Yes sir."

"Shortly after Guy Masters was arrested?"

"Yes sir."

"Splendid. Congratulations. I must say to all assembled here that in Detective Bernard, we, the residents of New York, seem to have a highly commendable public servant.

"As I understand your testimony, it seems that your partner, Officer Melo, took the lead in these proceedings. Is that correct?" Bernard didn't answer. "Let me help you out. At the door, when you first saw Guy Masters, it was Officer Melo who did most of the talking?"

"No sir."

"You both had equal time as it were?"

"We both talked."

"Well fine. But I believe you said that you thought Masters should be taken to the precinct for further questioning. Right?"

"Right."

Warren took him through every phase of the pickup and the ride to the precinct. Bernard was a perfect witness, always sure of himself, volunteering nothing. "I want to be sure about one thing, Bernard. Who read or informed the accused of his rights? You said he'd been so informed and that this was standard procedure. Now then, which of you read him his rights?"

Bernard shifted a bit. "Officer Melo read him his rights."

"Your Honor, I want to be quite clear about this.

103

You, Paul Bernard, did not inform the accused of his rights? That was done by Officer Melo?"

"Correct."

Bernard was excused. Melo was called to the stand. When Michaels had finished, Melo had substantiated Bernard. Then Warren took over.

"Now, Officer Melo, will you please recite those rights just as you did to the accused on the night in question?" As Melo began, Warren hit the button on his stopwatch. It was out of sight in his coat pocket.

"You have a right to remain silent. . ." He raced on. Warren thumbed the button and then produced the watch.

"Your Honor, that recitation took exactly thirteen seconds. I assume everyone in this room clearly heard and understood each word that Officer Melo uttered?"

Score one for him, Fred Michaels said to himself. And I saw it coming. . . .

"Now Officer Melo," Warren continued, "You were present at the interrogation of Guy Masters?"

"Yes sir."

"Where did it take place?"

"Our standard interrogation room."

"I have here a room plan of the precinct. In which of these rooms did you question the accused?"

Melo pointed to it.

"Would you say it was a well-ventilated room?"

"Not well-ventilated like outdoors. But remember, the door was open. There was a fan going. It was real cool in there. I had to put on my coat. It musta been about sixty to sixty-five degrees. Besides, it was a hot day. He was comfortable alright."

"Is that why you gave him urine to drink? And boiling hot water?"

Michaels was on his feet. "Objection!" Scott pulled at his sleeve. Warren moved in face-to-face with the witness.

"Under what conditions would you drink urine or boiling hot water?"

"None, sir." said Melo. "But we didn't do a thing like that. We treated him like a gentleman."

"And damn near broke his back?'"

"Objection!" yelled Michaels, up on his feet and approaching Melo. "There is no proof."

"That is all," Warren said quietly. Melo stepped down.

"I call as my next witness Donald Albright, the officer who took down Guy Masters's confession—as he dictated it," said Michaels with a glance toward Scott.

Allbright testified that the man was unsteady and his hand so shaky that he could write nothing.

Then Warren approached the witness.

"You mean you took over?"

"Yes sir."

"On the same pad on which Masters had been writing?"

"Why, yes."

"Did you retain what he wrote?"

"No sir."

"Why not?"

"Well, I was writing it. I began from the beginning again." The man floundered, knew he was right. What was the old fool getting at? He straightened in his seat, lowered his brows.

"Did you both use a ball-point pen?"

"He did. I used a nylon-tipped pen."

"Do you have that pad here, the one on which you took the confession?"

"No sir, I don't. It's back at the station house. I guess it's all used up by now. That was three months ago."

"But you do have the page on which you wrote the confession?"

"Is it the next sheet in the pad? The one after Masters wrote his own confession?"

"May I see the actual confession in Officer Allbright's handwriting?"

Michaels handed over the sheet of lined yellow paper.

Warren looked at it closely. "I don't see any indentation of writing on this second sheet transferred from the sheet which had been on top of it. If a man had written on the sheet just before this with a ballpoint pen, some impression of that writing would be apparent. This sheet is clean. I would like an adjournment to get an expert to make a test to see if this sheet bears any impression made upon it from the sheet above it."

Fred was back on his feet and permitting himself a slight show of impatience. "This is quite unnecessary, Your Honor. Witness has testified he used a nylon pen—very common these days—and, as everyone knows, these pens require little or no pressure. The flow of ink is copious."

"Nevertheless," Warren thundered, "some pressure, however slight, is involved, or even some microscopic transfer of ink from the top sheet to the under sheet. I demand an adjournment and the testimony of expert witness."

The judge looked sad. He doodled some lines on his pad. "Adjourned until tomorrow."

The next day, Warren introduced M. Cornelius Goldwater, a handwriting expert of thirty years experience covering more than five thousand cases of handwriting identification and related matters such as that brought up by Warren: that a nylon-tipped pen, while it might leave no impression, would nonetheless reveal its use.

"That's not entirely my point," Warren persisted. "What I want to know is this: Were there any traces on that sheet of impression such as might have been formed by a ball-point pen writing on the sheet above?"

"I found none."

"None whatever?"

"None."

"Then this is the first sheet of this pad?"

"It would seem so."

The next witness called by Fred was Officer Murphy, who stated the accused had been indeed permitted to make a telephone call and that he had spoken to someone. Warren doubted him.

"When did you permit the defendant to place this telephone call?"

Murphy said that it was within thirty minutes of his being booked at the station house.

"That would be on the night of May 12?"

"Yes sir."

"And to prove we were more than considerate," Murphy went on, "we let him dial long distance."

Warren smiled smugly at him, then turned to the judge. "I would like to introduce into evidence this computer tape from the New York Telephone Company recording all the completed long distance calls made from the station house telephone in that room. It has been brought here by Mr. Oberfeld from the accounting department of that corporation in an effort to obtain justice for my client. It conclusively proves he was not permitted to make his allowed telephone calls."

D. P. Scott had slipped in quietly as if to observe the last sword thrust in the bull ring. Now he plucked violently at Fred's sleeve. "For Christ's sake, object! He's trying to prove an illegally obtained confession!"

"I object!" Fred shouted from a seated position. Of course. Prove the confession was illegally obtained and what they had left was the button. Well, that plus the testimony of Julia McElroy, the hospital staff, and the girl's positive ID plus the cops' report would still sink the bastard. What was Warren up to? "That telephone company sheet only covers the twenty-four-hour period beginning at 11:00 P.M. of that night through the next night at the same hour. He could have called earlier or later!"

"It is not true, Your Honor!" shouted Warren. "If my worthy opponent will look, he will see it covers a forty-eight-hour period. There is no record of a completed call!"

"Your Honor," interrupted Fred, "we have no proof that the records cover the telephone he used, no proof that this record is accurate, or how it is kept. We have no proof of any of these issues. This telephone tape is complete hearsay—a stab in the dark to try and throw out a very, very legally obtained confession! Also, we have no evidence of how this computer tape is obtained by the telephone company!"

"Let the testimony stand," said the judge, and Warren returned smugly to his client.

"This is the one and only time you'll go on the stand. So go up there," Fred heard him whisper to Masters.

"I now call the defendant, Guy Masters, to the witness stand," he stated. Masters strode forward, swore to tell the truth and nothing but the truth, and began answering.

"When they found me at the door trying to find a place to go to the bathroom, they hit me on the forehead. They swung my back hard up against the wall and used a night stick to attack me. They hit my thigh with it, and my legs, and came up between them to hit my testicles. I almost fainted. Then the two policemen threw me into the back of the car and when we got to the station they tossed me out onto the sidewalk. They took me in and when I wanted to make a call, they yelled at me, and the line was busy and they wouldn't let me try again. Well... they shoved me hard onto a straight-backed chair, pulled a hot bright light down over my head and crowded around me, asked me questions, all of them at once. They sat around in a circle with this hot light on my head and they hit me all over my body. One guy said, 'Don't show any bruises.' They hurt my arm twisting it behind my back and they jumped on my feet. I was barefoot. Yes. They took my shoes and socks off. I don't know why. They trampled on my feet. They brought me piss to drink... and boilin' hot water, and they hit me behind the head, in the ribs. Then they left me alone for a couple of hours. Then they came back and hit me some more. I was hot and dizzy. I just kinda blanked out. They wouldn't give me any water."

There was a pause while he leaned over and dramatically poured himself some water which he drank thirstily—as if he had been denied it ever since the night he was describing.

"They called me an obscene name. They kept using obscene and dirty words."

"May I ask you to give me an example?" the judge requested.

Masters looked at him, grinned, and said, "Well,

they said I was a shithead, sir. I was also called a dirty motherfuckin' bastard."

"Mr. Masters," responded the judge after a pause, "did you confess voluntarily?"

"Your Honor, after what they did to me, I would have signed anything!"

"Before this arrest, had you been in a fist fight or an automobile accident?" Warren asked him. "Or in any situation where you suffered injuries of any kind?"

"No, I hadn't," Masters replied with emphasis.

Warren then developed that "unreasonable constraint and delay in arraignment," had taken place with an eight-hour lapse between the time he was arrested and the time he was brought down to court. Then when Michaels cross-examined Masters, according to instruction, he acted very polite and refused to get excited. He ended up by stating, "Mr. Michaels, if you had been there, I think you'd have been shocked at the way the police treated me."

"I will now call Dr. Rubin Levy to the stand," said Warren.

Dr. Levy, whose office was at 1019 Park Avenue, New York, stated yes, he had examined Guy Masters shortly after he had been released from the Tombs.

"I took X-rays of the man from head to foot after a thorough physical examination." He shook his head sadly. A man of fifty, he was bald and was extremely calm.

"And what did your examination and X-rays find?"

"That he had been severely beaten about the head, neck, shoulders, stomach, groin, and feet."

"Wow!" said Fred to himself.

"He had a black-and-blue welt the size of a baseball on his thigh. He had a large bruise mark on his groin near his penis. His right foot suffered severe damage

110

to the arch. One toe was broken. His neck had been consistently subjected to what we commonly call violent whiplash. The neck muscles and the muscles along his vertebrae were torn and stiffened. They were swollen. His right arm was black-and-blue along its entire length and his muscles were strained. He complained of an ache down his shoulders. The man had obviously been beaten. I considered placing him in a hospital."

Fred demanded to know how he could tell the black-and-blue marks were the result of a beating. "How do we know this so-called whiplash injury wasn't encountered in an automobile accident? Couldn't the bruises have been the result of something completely unrelated to this case?"

"The injuries were so cumulative it wa medically evident by their condition and amount to have been administered at the same time."

"How many visits did this man make to your office?"

"Three."

"And what did you prescribe in the way of medication which would treat a patient in this so-called condition?"

"Pain-killer. He was in severe pain for the first two weeks after the beating."

"Sir, I object. . ." began Michaels.

But the judge looked down on them all rather sadly, then began to speak: "Based on the evidence produced before me I find that there is far more than a reasonable doubt as to whether this evidence was legally procured."

He paused, looked at Fred again, and cleared his throat. "As a matter of fact, I find that the preponderance of the evidence indicates the confession was illegally procured. The fact that no completed telephone call was made when the police say that a call was completed . . . the fact that the eminent Dr. Levy found there were marks of severe brutality on this defendant which cannot be accounted for . . ."

He looked sternly at the assistant DA, "I accordingly find the confession to have been wrongfully obtained through means of threat and force and in violation of the defendant's constitutional rights. I accordingly suppress this evidence and direct that it not be used in the trial of this action."

Fred dragged himself to his feet, looked helplessly at Scott who strode off without a word.

Nine

It became a habit for Patricia to contact Fred and Fred to contact her when either encountered a problem in her series or in his case.

He called her, completely upset, and she responded. They met at their favorite cafe, Des Artistes. They ordered quietly, a bottle of Fume and the coq-au-vin. Charles, the owner, made a great fuss over her. "The distinguished television personality is with us again, non? Ah, you are so beautiful and so intelligent. It is not possible in one person!"

"This is my friend from the district attorney's office, Fred Michaels."

Fred took the elderly gentleman's hand. "You are the owner? You should be proud. This is a remarkable restaurant."

The older man shuffled away determined, he said, to make their meal a memorable one. Fred began after the first sip.

"There is something going on I don't like. When the

confession was thrown out, Warren didn't press for any more pretrial procedures."

"You mean he acts as if he has won a major point?"

"It's obvious he has. That judge was too lenient on him. For God's sake, getting a confession isn't a bed of roses.

"The cops have to use a certain amount of pressure —some threats. . ."

"All of which is illegal, right?"

"But why did he walk out with a big grin on his face with his arm over Masters's shoulder as if they had won something momentous? Sure, he goes to trial now without a confession facing him. But there is all that evidence."

While they ate, Warren shared a Schrafft's meal with Masters. They sat facing one another at Forty-seventh and Third waiting for the girl to bring them water and another knife. "I feel we should have a good talk, you and I. Every once in a while a defendant begins to wonder about his attorney's tactics —not that I have to explain mine—which might be worrying that young ADA."

"I think I'll have the swordfish," Masters said. He was studying the menu. "And some salad."

That upset the older man tremendously. The rapist sitting in front of him wasn't even listening!

"I basically don't like you, Masters. I think you raped the girl. I'm going to get you off. But before I go any further, I want to know one thing. Did you go traipsing back there the other night and scare the shit out of her or not? The cops have warned me. They were alerted. She said it was you. So out with it!"

Masters looked up, put down the menu, and said, "I may have gone by there, why?"

114

"You're stupid! Not only ungrateful, but a God-damned fool! You can lose what I have worked for all my life! If you had been caught there—anywhere near her—let alone listening at her door, you'd have been slapped away for twenty-five years to life! You are a fool and I have half a mind to withdraw from the case. You'll have a hell of a time ever getting another lawyer to handle this case. You tell me everything now. I mean *everything*. Begin!"

"Well, first of all, as I said to you I don't remember but I. . ."

"Talk!"

"What she said about what happened. I guess it must have . . . happened. I don't know. I never did anything like that before. . ."

"You guess it must have happened? You attacked that girl against her will and buggered her for a moment of sadistic pleasure, and then left her there to die. You forced yourself on her. That's a personal and vicious attack. And you *guess* it happened? You *are* stupid."

Masters got up. He was bigger all over and younger than his lawyer. He looked about ready to hit him. Then he seemed to think better of it. His breathing was heavy. "You're calling me names. What do you want from me?"

Warren had risen, too. Now he sat down and slowly sipped at his water, his heart resuming its normal beat. He knew he had goaded Masters because he hated what he had to do for him, protecting the right of even a rapist to legal counsel.

"Forget it! You raped her and I'm getting you off. Forget it. You'll walk down those steps, out of court into the street . . . and you'll hit the sidewalk a free man."

"Well, why should five minutes of fun put me behind bars for twenty-five years?"

Masters sat in a huge courtroom at 100 Centre Street. Warren had said the trial would actually begin. The "People" would gather to try to put him away for something the People said he had done months ago. Warren had told him he had been purposely stalling "like a vaudeville trouper milking his jokes and refusing to leave stage." Now he himself was near being a celebrity. The whole scene had changed. Instead of being a nobody—now he was a somebody. The papers were helping and so was that woman on TV. She acted like she was running for election or something. And so his trial would make the news of the decade. And the girl?

Masters knew he had to face her and was building up a hatred. Soon, like him, she would have to walk into the courtroom and sit over there. His lawyer had told him so. He wondered what was going on downstairs—or wherever it was that the judge had sent the two lawyers to pick the jury.

"Select the jury downstairs!" Rosenman had intoned solemnly and risen as if he had, with those words, evoked some judicial charm which would bring justice to all within his hearing. Then, as though leaving a well-turned garden, he walked away.

Fred had looked at Warren. Warren had looked at Fred. Now they had gone off somewhere, and he had been told to wait.

He had to find the men's room. It was sudden. As if fear had thrown a switch. He guessed he could go where he wished; so he stood up and walked into the hallway of the courthouse. It was long, high, and well-lighted.

In the corridor coming toward him, just leaving the ladies' room, was Susan Landress. How should he act? What did a rapist do when confronted afterwards in a courthouse by the girl he was accused of raping? Should he act the innocent?—"How nice to see you again? Sorry about that"—all that sort of thing? Or should he stumble past her mumbling insanely to himself? The intervening months had changed him. He actually thought of her now as a kind of sweetheart. And here she was not ten feet away, just as desirable, just as off in the clouds and obviously completely indifferent to what had happened between them. She moved rapidly to get it over with, her eyes straight ahead as if he didn't exist. He was five feet away from the person he had beaten, attacked with his teeth, torn naked, and abused. She walked primly past him, a breath of perfume, a flush upon her cheeks, blonde hair aflutter, and he didn't blink, reach out, attempt to stop her. He held his breath. She was past, gone into history. They were two people who hadn't known one another except in a law book, a file somewhere at his lawyer's office. He turned to take one last long look at what he had once so completely possessed and he knew in a flash that he had never really had her. It had been a complete and violent conquest, but he hadn't touched the girl. He hadn't reached her. She disappeared in the court.

Ten men walked toward him discussing a case loudly. They walked in pairs. They formed a wall between him and the courtroom as he spun about, a sudden need to see her, observe her, know whether in his criminal act he had had any effect upon her at all.

He couldn't have gone through all that and left nothing. The men gathered at the door and started in. He waited as they slowly, one by one, went ahead of him. The last two were speaking. "Did you see the girl that just went in here ahead of us?"

"Yes," replied the other.

"A real beauty!"

Masters returned to his seat. What did those men really know about her!

In finishing her previous broadcast, Patricia had said: "The victim in a rape case is always better off if the jury includes more men than women. Do you find this strange? There are two reasons, I presume. First: Men are gallant and very 'straight' when in the spotlight—let's call them a race of hard hats or Puritans, no matter how they feel themselves. The woman who is raped is a victim. The male feels called upon to come to her aid. The second reason is women naturally feel that the victim could have done something to protect herself. I am studying a case right now in which the victim wandered aimlessly into a park. It could be considered a bit of bad judgment. A woman would think, 'I never would have done that!'

"When the jury selection starts, you'll find the DA looking for men and the defense looking for women.

"Patricia Rankin, for Group One News."

The jury impaneling clerk had placed two hundred names inside a large, six-sided pine tub. He could rotate the tub by means of a huge handle. Then, from one of the sides which opened on hinges, he could select the names of fifty persons who would make up the jurors first called. Some of those in the room would be asked to serve on the jury; others would be designated the two alternates. They were the persons who would be called upon to make a decision about the case in which they would judge the guilt of a man accused of Rape One and Sodomy One.

When the first fifty names were pulled from the drum, read out, and placed in position upon a board, they were told to separate from the others and take seats on the opposite side of the room. Then the judge began his speech:

"We acknowledge, ladies and gentlemen, that we all have prejudices. It is nearly impossible to exist today, under the constant barrage of the printed word and those heard over our televisions and radios, and not to subconsciously form some set opinions which we hardly admit to ourselves, but which do exist. The law knows this. And as hard as it is to face one's own degree of fairness, we who uphold the law for you, the people, depend upon the jury process in our work, and know it to be a democratic system par excellence, that is, without peer. However, to make it work, I have to ask you certain questions. I do not mean to be personal or to pry into your private affairs, nor am I simply curious. I must find out if there is any potential bias involved and whether you have any set opinions which would make it impossible for you to be fair in this case."

Then one by one he spoke to each of the fifty persons asking questions, he said, which were only intended to help make this determination. Warren followed him.

They were asked had they ever been convicted of a crime, did they know the judge, the accused, or the DA, or anyone in their families. They were probed, explored, interrupted, quizzed. Those who replied satisfactorily remained, while those who didn't were excused.

"Do you know what rape is?" asked Warren of a middle-aged man who worked as a lineman for Consolidated Edison.

"I sure do," he replied with a laugh. "But I don't know why it's necessary today."

Betty Smollers, an employee from the Board of Education, was asked, "Have you ever seen an erect penis?" Warren stood in front of the prim little lady with a serious face. And in response to Michaels's disapproval he went on to state: "The question is relevant. This woman may be subjected to worse than this before we are through with her. But as to my question, there is much medical consideration being given to the fear engendered by the sight of the male organ on the part of women. If this woman is familiar with the sight of a flaccid penis she knows it is harmless, whereas if she is confronted with an erect penis she may consider the man has a fearsome weapon."

"Well," stated Betty Smollers, "on the contrary. I think they are rather. . .er, ridiculous! From the ones I have seen."

Mrs. Bertha Klausmeyer, who had come down in autumn to make certain her name was on the jury list, shifted from her position in line and fluttered when she was to be questioned. She pecked away at the answers in short bursts as first Michaels, from dead center before her, and later Warren, from far to her right, shot questions at her like seeds which she caught in midair.

Warren knew women usually find reasons why the victim could have avoided the inevitable rape or think the girl who was raped "asked for it." He was anxious to have her. Finally, he asked, "Do you think rape is possible ma'am?"

She seemed not to hear, so he repeated the question. She looked at Michaels, who stared back, finding nothing objectionable in the interrogation. "Why yes," she said. "It happens all the time. I knew a woman whose husband raped her every night."

The next one caused controversy. It seemed that less than three years ago Gertrude Marlsovitch had herself been raped. "This man came to the door with my husband's blue suit. Only Herbert don't have no blue suit at the cleaners. This young man, about six feet and blond, he closed the door and went to the telephone to call his boss who told him we don't trade with him, he should have his head examined; so he grabs me, right around the throat. I screamed, so he chokes. My, does he choke. Then he gets himself excited, you can believe me. He rapes me. Then he leaves. I ran to the window when he left and took down his license plate. He leaves this blue suit so we trace him. He is in jail now for twenty years." Of course, both sides rejected her.

The fifth juror had been seated by lunch break. Neither attorney found anything to challenge in a retired school teacher. She gave her age as sixty-six, her sex as female, and her religion as "God fearing." She said she knew what rape was, didn't wander about the streets after 2:00 A.M. like the TV show advised, but she did get up and take a 'constitutional' before 8:00 A.M. "whether there is a rapist out there or not!" She was not going to be robbed of her walk with Pepe, her poodle.

A black woman in her thirties told them she was a housewife, had never been arrested, that her husband worked for a band, was on a "gig" on a boat cruise, that she had a brother "on the force" upstate, and that she knew about rape.

"I live in Harlem," she advised them with a grim smile.

They accepted Mrs. George L. Stockwell. She sat perfectly straight with serious brown eyes and a somber mouth as if the event was to start now that she had arrived.

Short, wide, and fussy, Mrs. Howard J. Koch said she owned a coiffing salon and that she never had any trouble with the police about her license to operate, nor had her late husband—until they killed him.

"Killed him?" asked Fred. "Who? The police?"

"He ran a big policywheel. The 'Man' had him bumped off. I never missed him. Howie was no lover. A contract was out on him and I warned him. They never got the men who done it, but I don't care."

Neither attorney cared for her as a prospective juror.

"Do you believe in women's lib?" Warren asked the next woman, about thirty-five, blond, and wearing a see-through blouse. Her short hair was brushed back, her mouth and face unmarked by makeup, and her bare arms, shoulders, and legs were a deep tan. She was healthy, ebullient, and showed big white teeth when he asked her the question.

"It all depends," she said, "who's involved."

"I only wanted to know whether you felt a woman could be raped," he smiled at her, coming closer and peering into her bold brown eyes.

"Sure. By anyone—even a woman."

He walked away with a grin growing on his face. He ran a hand through his white hair and approached her again.

122

"Then rape isn't a male-instigated crime against a woman but, according to you, can be perpetrated between any two humans?"

"Sure. Why not? A woman might rape a man, too." She looked brightly about as if advising them of some new discovery. "I mean a woman coming on strong with, say, a weapon at his throat can rape a man, can't she?"

"The definition of rape places the crime against men only for good reason. An unwilling male cannot complete the act of coitus."

"Bullshit!"

She was excused. Next was a sweet young housewife who said her husband worked for the telephone company, that he had insisted on her accepting jury duty because she was always complaining she was bored at home.

"Very refreshing," said Fred. "I wished more citizens accepted jury duty as exciting."

"We will try to keep you amused," said Warren.

After acceptance of three elderly ladies on Social Security who had respectively taught (a) English (b) history, and (c) her grandchildren how to make a Scandinavian dish called "Levsa," jury selection was over.

The night before the trial began Fred met Patricia for their final consultation. He was extremely worried and said so.

She patted the sofa. "Come over here and sit with me. I feel in a consoling mood."

Her rambling apartment was done with what she called "remnants of my life in the breeding area near Darien, Connecticut." The high ceiling, informal decor, and casual atmosphere made Fred feel at ease.

He moved next to her, his arm behind her on the back of the couch, his cigarette in one hand.

She asked, "What is it?"

"I'm a very sensitive guy, I guess, for a man." He stopped, realizing how stupid that sounded. "But I can't help feeling strange about the people we let sit on that jury." He looked down at her, her eyes more brown than he had noticed. "You know how antiquated, yet correct, our jury selection system is. We get the middle or lower class mind usually. Others, like you and me (if I was available) would get out of it somehow. Great! We're informed, aware citizens, while those dumbbells. . .!" He made a wild gesture with his hand, the fingers splaying out. Her eyes followed them. "They become our peers. Our peers! Why, a jury of our peers would have had ten years more education, would be well-read and well-traveled, and wouldn't sit every day and night glued to the boob tube—oh, excuse me—all night!"

"You think they'll react typically."

He took her hand quickly. It was warm. She didn't pull away, just looked across the room at the huge mirror over the table on which she had spread every conceivable publication.

"Look at me, will you?" he asked.

He saw something in her face, her little oval face with the divine complexion and the pursed lips as if she had just asked a huge audience a question and was waiting for the answer. . .and he answered it by pulling her toward him. Their lips were inches apart. She kissed him, then quickly pushed him away and leapt to her feet. "You have a trial tomorrow. You're all tensed up and you think. . .well, your mind isn't on that girl as much as you believe. Here, let me fill your glass."

124

He beat her to the narrow kitchen and took her free hand, spun her around, and held her very tightly.

Over her head, he said, "I'm nothing. . .just a nobody compared to you. You rather frighten me. I can't feel like a man should. You know. . .in charge. Well, after I win this case—that is, in a week or so—and that girl is back in society and part of it as a full-fledged and happy member, then I'll feel I have accomplished something."

She stepped back, free of his arms.

"You're just the greatest guy in the world! And don't you ever forget it. You're a man, too, the kind a woman like me likes. Because you care. I don't ask you to be anything more than what you are now—tonight and well, ever!"

Later that night, Fred felt very happy and confident. He wasn't worried any longer about the case or about anything.

"I know you were worried about her and maybe even about the entire system," Patricia had said at the door. "But go home now, get some rest, and knock 'em dead tomorrow."

He had walked briskly to the corner and hailed a cab with the command of a man who knew that, no matter how heavy the traffic, that cab would stop! He smiled and realized something terribly important had just happened to him.

Ten

"Is the prosecution ready?"

Fred nodded confidently. The trial had begun. He sat next to Donald Scott, who said he'd make an appearance for the formality of it.

"Is the defense ready?"

Warren said he was ready. Masters sat with head held high, his face expressionless, as instructed. He wore a dark suit and tie and looked like a corporation lawyer who had dropped in to represent an insurance company. The pair looked very respectful and indeed seemed ready.

"Call your first witness, Mr. Michaels."

A middle-aged man with mild blue eyes, bent shoulders, and a grey flannel suit walked to the stand. He said he was Dr. Hugh Margate and that he was associated with the hospital complex at Sixty-third and the East River.

The questioning began. Susan sank low in her uncomfortable wooden chair. Michaels stood before the doctor and asked him about himself. "I am licensed to practice in this state. Yes, I have held my license thirteen years since graduating from medical school in this city." Then he was asked, "Are you familiar with the test necessary to discover whether a woman has had sexual intercourse?"

"I am."

"On May 13 did you have occasion to examine Susan Landress for this purpose?"

"Yes I did."

"What were the circumstances of this examination?"

"She came into the hospital with one of our nurses and she told the receptionist. . ."

But Warren interrupted, "Your Honor, I respectfully object to that answer. As the Court well knows, that is hearsay and Susan Landress is sitting right here. She can tell us what she told him."

Fred turned back to Dr. Margate. "What did she tell you?"

"She appeared very distraught and upset. She was almost hysterical, but a woman—a nurse with her—said she had been raped. I took her into the examination room."

"Did you then cause an examination to be made and did you conduct this test? Did you examine her microscopically and. . ."

"I examined her and found the presence of spermatozoa in the vaginal tract."

"Based on your experience, do you have any way of knowing how old those spermatozoa were?"

"I do. We determined they were present no longer than twenty four hours. . .maybe less."

"Is it your opinion that this woman. . .had been raped?"

127

"Objection!" Warren was up. "There is no evidence whatsoever here. . ."

"Sustained."

"Did you find any marks on her body?"

Margate thought a moment, then looked at the judge, then back to his questioner. "Why yes."

"What did you find?"

"Abundant contusions, abrasions, and lacerations. A sign of teeth marks on the left breast."

Susan had her hand over her face. She was blushing but she couldn't help it. They were discussing her body as if it belonged to some cadaver. She was a living human being, a woman with feelings. Sure, she had had cuts and bruises, but the way that horrible little man discussed her, it sounded as if she again was just so much meat on a butcher's block. As if the rape itself hadn't been humiliating enough.

"Can you tell us where you found these lacerations, abrasions, and contusions?"

"I found bruises on her left thigh above the knee and one on her lower abdomen above the pubis. Those two were the size of a half dollar. On her inner right thigh I found a series of bruises probably inflicted by strong fingers as if coitus interfemur had been attempted. I found a long scratch which had been bleeding running from her labia majora to about four inches above her pubis. What seemed like fingernail scratches had torn skin the size of a dime on her right hip, and the lower portion of both buttocks bore deep purple bruises I recognized as made by the grasping hands of her assailant. Her left breast was bruised and reddened and showed the distinct mark of incisor teeth about her nipple area. She had apparently been bitten, for they were the marks left by a person biting another viciously. It must have been very painful."

"Did you photograph these marks or the areas described?"

"No sir. It is not our custom."

"Thank you. Now, Doctor, please tell me, did the victim come to the hospital of her own free will?"

"Certainly. She made no objections if that's what you mean. A nurse from the hospital found her. A Julia McElroy, whom I know. I verbally reported my findings to Mrs. McElroy, who remained there during the examination."

"Were there any other marks on her body?"

"Her face seemed red...maybe swollen. I didn't examine the tissue. I didn't think it strange, though."

"Why?"

"A man attacking a woman often strikes her face."

"Based on your experience, had the woman had sexual intercourse within the past twenty-four hours?"

"Yes."

"What other indications of an attack did you find?"

"None, other than the teeth marks on her left breast which I could not miss seeing."

Susan watched the reporters taking this all down. How awful! Guy Masters sat there straight and almost proud, his black hair agleam in the light. His face was that of an innocent man—eyebrows held high—almost amused at the evidence—aloof. The solemn judge peered down, the twelve jurors seated, waiting, anxious to hear more of her terrifying night and evidence of her degradation, her body being used by a stranger.

Dr. Margate had been consulting some papers. Now Michaels asked him, "I see that you are referring to something in writing as you tell us of your examination."

"It's my medical report upon which I noted the observations of my examination."

"May I ask that they be introduced for identification marked 'People's Exhibit One?'"

"Is there any objection?" asked the judge.

"No objection," said Warren.

"No further questions," snapped Michaels.

Warren was permitted to read the medical report, which he looked over very carefully. Then he stood up and walked to the witness.

"Is it possible for a woman to inflict wounds such as these . . . upon herself, Dr. Margate?"

There was an intaking of breath. The judge grimaced. Michaels started to get up, then sat down.

The doctor looked across at Warren with deadly seriousness. "I don't think it would be possible, sir."

"Perhaps she ran into a desk—the corner of a desk. Or maybe she used an. . .instrument or vibrating machine upon herself. Or. . ."

"Objection."

"Doctor," asked Warren, "before coming to court here today, did you consult with the district attorney?"

"Yes, I did."

"Before coming into court here today, did you go over your medical records?"

"I did."

"While consulting with the district attorney and going over those records, did you have any independent recollection of this situation or what happened to this particular girl?"

"No, I have hundreds of them every week. How could I?"

130

"Then doctor, these medical records form the sole foundation of your recollection of the incident?"

"Yes, they do."

"Doctor, I see nothing here about a bite on the breast. Could she have actually bitten her own breast?"

"Objection!" said Michaels, in a disgusted tone of voice, looking at Warren as if he was totally nauseated by his tactics.

"Warren is leading up to something," whispered Scott. "He will try to discredit the doctor somehow."

Warren held the medical papers before the doctor.

"Sir," he said quietly, "I see no notation of the bite made by a person unknown upon the lady's breast in these reports."

The doctor reached for the sheets, looked hurriedly up and down. "Take your time. Read them carefully. We are in no hurry," said Warren.

Dr. Margate handed the papers back to him. "I guess I didn't write it in the report."

Warren seemed shocked. He walked quickly toward him. "Now, wait a minute, doctor!" He paused. "Do you mean that although you testified you observed a brutal, sadistic bite, and you examined the patient carefully to determine whether she had been raped or not, and although your report included lacerations, abrasions, and contusions as small as dimes, you did not make a note of an obvious bite on her breast?"

"No sir, apparently I didn't."

Fred was on his feet objecting.

"Let the doctor's testimony stand," said Scott now up and at the side of his assistant. "We would like the medical report to stand—without the bite!" he said to the judge.

But Warren wasn't finished with him. "How long have you been in practice, Dr. Margate?"

"That's repetitious!" barked the annoyed Fred.

"Thirteen years, sir."

"May I presume that in a case of this seriousness you would be very thorough and that normally you would not forget such things?"

The man's face brightened. Then, as if to justify himself, he said, "Never! I've never forgotten as serious a thing as this before."

"Fine." said Warren. "How many women do you examine for rape in a week, sir?"

The doctor thought a moment. "We get about twenty-five to thirty examinations a week!"

"Then are you saying that although you have examined more than seven hundred women during the six months since Susan Landress was there and, that in a case of this seriousness you never—I quote you, sir —never forget such things, you are still certain that it was her breast which someone had bitten?"

There was general laughter in the courtroom. Susan reddened and sank lower in her chair.

"Dr. Margate," Warren continued, "you stated that you found a series of bruises probably inflicted by strong fingers as if coitus interfemur had been attempted. How do you know this? What evidence do you have to sustantiate the bruise marks were made by 'strong fingers'?"

"I can tell."

"Were you there? Did you witness an attempt at coitus interfemur, whatever that is?"

"It's when. . ."

"Never mind, Dr. Margate."

"Well, she had finger marks."

"You cannot prove that."

132

"Well, it was rape because she told me it was rape!" he blurted out.

"Hitler told us he wanted peace, judge," Warren began, loudly. "I move that this be stricken. This is complete hearsay."

"This man is equating the doctor with Hitler!" cried Fred, angrily. All was noise and turmoil. The clerk yelled for order. The Judge gaveled sharply, and nobody noticed Susan Landress as she sank slowly into unconsciousness. A clerk leapt forward to catch her.

Susan awoke and found herself on a leather couch, her head hanging uncomfortably off it, with a woman guard bending over her. The guard's uniform smelled musty, but her face was pleasant. "How is she?" a man asked from the doorway.

"How are you?" the woman asked, holding Susan's hand. "Can you be driven home?"

Susan was on her feet. Invalidism was not for her. She had had enough of that with her mother. Steadying herself on the arm of the heavy-set woman in blue, she brushed off her clothes, then checked her hair.

The man at the door said the DA's office would get her a cab.

Later, in her studio apartment, she started washing the dirty dishes. The sink was a mess. It always gave her a chance to unwind when she had household chores to do. It had been easier on the Coast, no problems like the ones she had now, and that's where she had determined to avoid pill-taking or drugs to solve her problems.

The cushions needed fluffing, the ashtrays and empty glasses had to be cleaned and returned to place. The day's events were closing in on her and she wanted to lie down flat on the open couch and erase the memory.

All the talk about her breast in court forcefully brought home how much, how overly concerned other people were with themselves as bodies, whereas, she, a child of the Pacific Ocean surf, was not. Lying there, dreamily watching the ceiling turn into a day when the surf was up, Susan tried to think of when she or a girl friend might have ever displayed the least self-consciousness about daily life in a bikini or brief nudity when the blue sky, the hot sand, and privacy permitted. Oh sure, there were the types anywhere who spent hours getting a tan, never entering the water except to dab a little on for a better color. But they weren't her friends, her peers. Her boy friends had been sports-minded, always in the water, red-eyed from it at night, living in it all day. There was an openness about physicality that made it Spartan, clean, and when dirty old men gave it another twist, as they sometimes had done, she and her gang had tapped their heads, laughed, and run away.

But Susan knew she was in another world now and that she couldn't laugh away the twelve jurors, the old judge, and what that man Warren was trying to do to her.

It was terribly upsetting to realize that at her age she had to do an about-face and begin to think and act like a different person, no longer as she pictured herself, carefree, easy-going, comfortable with her body and happy about it. Discussions in her school had been healthy, she remembered. She had reached womanhood without fireworks or a national holiday. She had met the oncoming evidence of her change from girl to woman with enthusiasm but with no emotion. Susan felt that her womanhood was her business—and hers alone. Now her body was being kicked about in a man-filled court, subjected to verbal analysis. It made her sick!

Practically asleep, but unable to relax completely, Susan stared at the ceiling. She was taking too many blows. She couldn't see how she could cope with any more. She was slowly becoming very confused by it all. There was a strong stance she would have to take, or like a lost swimmer in a hurricane, she would finally give up and drown. The sense of drowning, the cutting off of one's breath, the filling of lungs, was not unlike what had almost happened to her in Malibu, when the big wave caught her, the board had flipped, hit her head, and she had been pulled out by quick-thinking friends. Even while going under, her feet had been cross-kicking, and her second personality, the thing that lived inside her which said, "Fight!" had carried her on until the help came.

Why not now? Certainly she was in as much danger. And while no strong-armed friends seemed near, her self-reliance must grow or she would be swallowed up. The kind of talk men used in respect to her, and their laughter in that male-dominated court-room, had shocked her. For the first time it became apparent that she must not just fight for herself, to put that man away for what he had done to her as an individual, as a woman, but she must fight for what it might do to correct the injustice of the things that any woman faced. All rape victims, whether they had the stupidity or guts to go to the law, would be faced with similar male attitudes.

Anne had mentioned a gun.

"If I were you, sister, I'd take my gun and next time I saw the bastard, I'd shoot him!"

Her gun.

Susan rose slowly and walked to where Anne had told her she always hid the revolver—a little .32 palm gun which she, as a stewardess, couldn't keep on her person though she faced skyjackers. She had said, "But I'll carry it in this bloody city, license or not. I mean to retain my choices when it comes to sex!"

There it was, black and evil.

Susan gingerly touched it. It was cold. It lay on a folded white slip making a dent in the nylon, cold and ugly.

She couldn't.

Slowly, she closed the drawer. It was nice to know it was there. But that wasn't the way. Not violence. A rapist had used violence. The victim would use reason.

Like someone slow to anger, she had crossed the line. From now on they would have a woman to deal with who knew what she wanted. She'd show them. She'd go through with it for all women. All the way.

She felt happy, almost euphoric; then suddenly she was asleep.

Three months ago she had started looking for another job through the Wallace Nelson Employment Agency. They had been most solicitous and had sent her to three big Madison Avenue advertising agencies where the girl had told her, "You'll get swallowed up by personnel and earn a decent living without making waves."

Having been chosen to work in the copy pool as an assistant account executive steno, Susan had felt anonymity had reached its zenith. She had begun living her life without visibility, keeping as low a profile as possible, and when the judge recessed the court the next morning, because it was someone's birthday, she went up to Bloomingdale's and began buying dresses she would never have chosen before. Part of her nonperson approach to her new role was to be 'everywoman,' yet herself. So she chose things a little bit big and a little bit late in style. In the job that first week no one had spoken to her going or coming until they handed her her first check and the paymaster had said, "I haven't seen you around here at all. I'm so glad a woman of your type is working with Bannister, Kerner and Ayers." She had deposited her $96.65 with a smile.

Fred Michaels didn't have to tell her how to dress in court or how to think about her problem as a complainant anymore. He had a "thinking woman" on his hands.

Eleven

Fred had instructed her to come to the courtroom no later than ten the next morning. "Be a little early. I am putting Officer Peter Melo on the stand. It is always good, I am told, if an arresting officer can see the victim while he testifies. He feels justified in putting the accused away. He gets sharp, gives explicit testimony. He doesn't feel alone up there against the rapist, feels vindicated for putting the man in jail."

Amid subway noise, stench, crowds pushing, Susan moved up the stairway to the street angry at the hurrying, indifferent world for treating her this way, for making her go through this ordeal because of her body.

She looked up the steps leading inside the Criminal Courts Building and the courtroom. They were foreboding, like an insurmountable mountain peak. At the top, up there, under those columns were doorways leading to a huge, high-ceilinged chamber.

Winding stairways or elevators would take you to the proper floor. Inside a stifling, closed room paneled in light walnut she would sit for weeks waiting. People would come and go. Witnesses like the doctor, like the policeman, would discuss the rape—her rape and her victimization, another statistic for a reporter, another headline for the article she saw on the front page of the paper on the newstands she had passed. And when it was all over, what? She clamped her jaw and started climbing. Was justice up there? Another two steps. Up there was Guy Masters, free. Up there —another step—was his lawyer. What could he possibly do or say to prove his man innocent? Two steps, three, four—thousands more to go. She was determined to make it.

Warren, as he said, "didn't give one hoot in hell now" whether his man was innocent or not. He had already dismissed as beneath him the idea of asking for a lesser plea. It was unnecessary. His man could "cop out" by getting a three month sentence for "simple assault." It would clear the court and move things along. It was better than twenty-five years. Watching Masters at the water fountain, he knew he could get him off entirely. Yet, he would have to counsel him again on his manner and appearance.

He walked over to him. Masters looked up, brushing water from his lips with the back of his hand. "Listen to me, it's important. I want you to stop hunching your shoulders like a muscle-bound truck driver . . . and don't hold your head up so high. You simply have to look humble and think more of the impression you are making on others. Take the jury, for example. You'll be in court while this little shy grieved girl will tell the twelve jurors how she stumbled all bewildered into the park where you grabbed her, tore off her clothes, and raped her. They will listen to her speak through tears and sobs—and then they'll look over at you. She undoubtedly will be instructed to cry at that moment."

Just then Susan Landress passed, small and forlorn, without a sign of recognition.

"At that point I want you to be looking directly at her. Right into her face. Even if she is crying and pointing at you. I want you to sit solidly and comfortably at ease in your seat but not slouching! I want your shoulders down and back against the bench. I want your head set straight with no jutting jaws or gritting of teeth or show of anger. Just a stare—a common, ordinary, garden-variety look at another person. I want you to be the accused who is being accused unjustly but I don't want surprise, innocence! Remember we all know the charges. Get in there, now, and remember, don't be obvious or too guileless."

"Now that it's . . . under way, Mr. Warren, are we goin' to win?"

Warren feigned shock. "It never occurs to me I won't. But . . . this Michaels."

"Yeah?"

"Too confident . . . strange tactics. Building up to something he is sure about . . . absolutely certain will work. Acting like a winner already. Though. . . ." He thought for a minute. "Maybe he's just young; doesn't know any better. On the other hand. . ."

"What?"

"Maybe there are little things I should have done."

"Like . . . a bribe?"

"Oh, for Chris' sake! Like that . . . bartender I could have examined. Maybe he knows something important which places you at the crime. I should have. I really should have examined him. Why else is he here, looking so smart and smiling all around if he hasn't been told, and rehearsed, and groomed to pop the big score? What is it he has on . . . you?"

"Me? Nothing. Not a thing. . ."

Warren seemed satisfied. He led the way in and down the aisle. He knew he would have to be about as clever as his reputation made him out to be. First he'd take that arresting officer and make little pieces out of him. He sat down and noticed his client had become smaller in the seat next to him. Good.

Guy Masters began getting worried. It had been a terrible letdown to see through Warren. So he wasn't exactly the clever old fox they said he was? He'd forgotten an important examination. The bartender, eh? The bartender? Masters sat low in the seat and tried not to look brutal, like a man who could rape a little thing like the girl in the corner over there. What did the bartender know? He tried to forget the scene before him, the intonation of the clerk calling the room for order, telling people to take their seats, the entry of the black-robed judge, the shuffling of papers. He went back to the night he had stood before that bartender and downed whiskey after whiskey. But try as he could, he couldn't bring that part of the evening into focus. Worried, not knowing why, he looked across the aisle at the victim. She sat in the corner, plainly dressed, head high, her long blond hair pinned up, her feet neatly pulled back under the seat, the image of innocence. He couldn't believe it wasn't all a dream. That girl over there was trying to put him into jail! Away for life! And his lawyer had forgotten something important, had left him with no protection!

Officer Peter Melo was on the stand. His clean uniform, hair cut short, and straightforward blue eyes personified law enforcement. He had been cautioned to get a good night's sleep, be alert, and answer only the question asked without volunteering. He would prove the defendant had been arrested for breaking and entering, or "an attempt."

"Did you have occasion to see the defendant on the night of May 12?" he was asked.

Fred was obviously enjoying every minute of it, dancing on the precipice of objection and cross-examination with all the bravado of a tightrope walker.

"I did." Melo looked stern like a lawman.

"When and where, please?"

"The defendant was bustin' in a door at this building where there is a bar, near the corner of Sixty-third and Second. On that night about—about 1:00 A.M., it was a locked door!"

"And what did you do?"

"I arrested him."

"That is all. Your witness!" Fred had been quick, to the point. He had proven the defendant was there that night, at that time, and had been booked for attempted breaking and entry. Next!

Warren was up. "Have you ever had to go to the bathroom so badly you would break down a door to do it? Have you ever had to go so acutely you couldn't stand it?" He stood facing Peter Melo with a deadly stare, brows down, and his shock of white hair agleam under the overhead chandeliers.

Fred had stood up at the first sentence and was now shouting his objections to the line of questioning which he termed "highly irrelevant, Your Honor."

But the judge shook his head. "No, I'll permit it."

"Officer Melo?" repeated Warren, "Have you ever

had to go to the toilet so badly, you'd try to break down a door to get in?"

Melo thought for a minute and said, "No, I ain't."

"Officer Melo," he went on, "how old are you?"

"I'm thirty-one years old."

"And during all that time you never got ... er, caught short?"

"No sir."

"Did you serve in the Armed Forces?"

"I did my two years."

"Always near a convenient toilet?"

"Sure."

"Where did you serve?"

"In Nam. I was there six months."

"Never caught short? Always near a john?"

"That's it."

"Did you describe Mr. Masters as forcing a locked door?"

"Yes, that's what he was doin'."

"Did you find any burglary tools on him?"

"What's that again?"

"Did you find a jimmy, a hammer, a wrench, dummy keys?"

"No, we did not."

"Did Masters advise you why he was trying to break in that door without benefit of any tools—but by just using his hands?"

"We stopped him from gettin' in there. He didn't have to tell us why. That was private property."

"After you stopped him, did he have an explanation?"

"Yes. He said he had to take a leak. That's what he said."

"Did you investigate to discover whether there is actually a toilet facility inside that door?"

"Yes. I went in there later."

"What for?"

"To—take a leak, sir. And to keep the suspect under my surveillance."

"And how far away is the toilet inside that door?"

"Just inside, sir."

"When you went in there to keep him under surveillance, what did he do and what did you do?"

"We both took a leak, sir."

"That is all."

Warren walked back to the table and smiled. He acted like a winner. Now he was addressing the judge and the other lawyer.

What was Warren saying? Something about "the interest of time." Masters bent forward to catch his words.

"In the interest of time. . ." he heard the lawyer say in his loud voice, "I am willing to stipulate that this part of the testimony regarding the arrest will conform to the facts testified to by Officer Melo." And then the black detective, Paul Bernard, stepped down from the witness stand where he had not had to testify. At the same time, Masters could see the bartender, that smiling bastard, getting his feet under him, all set to walk down the aisle and stand up before the clerk and swear to tell the truth, nothing but the truth, so help him God, and then sit in that armchair up there and describe things Warren should have questioned him about.

"Call Joseph Cartolla to the stand," said Fred.

Masters's heart sank and his breath came short. The head lawyer, the older man, Donald Scott, was going to question Cartolla. It was that important.

Scott stood before the witness and asked, "Have you had occasion to see the accused before?"

144

"Yes." Cartolla's voice boomed out.

"Where?"

"In my bar."

"When?"

"On May 12 at about midnight."

"And what was he doing in your bar?"

Masters's heart stopped. He began to shake. His legs jerked spasmodically. Warren put out a hand, but he began fidgeting, moving this way and that, unmindful of his actions. His hand went to his collar. He needed air!

"He was drinkin' whiskey, sir," came the answer.

"And what else was he doing besides drinking whiskey?" asked Scott, making each word count, obviously leading the man to the expected answer—an answer which would explain the previous question and bring down the ceiling.

During the past five minutes, ever since the prosecution had called Joseph Cartolla, Warren had been bothered, nagged by a vague discomfort about the bartender being called to the stand. For some reason he shouldn't be up there—or allowed to testify against his client. What was it? Then he remembered, just as the question was put asking what else his client had been doing at the bar, that night, right after the rape.

He stood up and shouted almost instinctively. "Objection, Your Honor! That witness cannot answer any further questions!"

Fred asked, "Why not? He has been sworn in. You have known of his appearance here."

"Your Honor," repeated Warren, ignoring Michaels because some inner sense said get that man off the stand quickly, "I ask that the jury be excused and that they leave the room while I answer Mr. Michaels's question."

The judge said, "Mr. Warren I presume you have a valid reason; so in the interest of preventing a mistrial, I excuse the jury." After they had filed out the judge asked for an explanation.

The button testimony he was about to get from Cartolla could never have been anticipated by the defense, Scott reasoned. What in thunder was Warren up to? He could never have guessed how damaging the bartender's words were about to have been.

Warren stood up.

"It is the opinion of the defense counsel that, but for the alleged illegal confession previously extracted from the defendant under the most questionable circumstances, the prosecution would never have learned under any circumstances, directly or indirectly, of the identity of this witness, Joseph Cartolla, Your Honor, much less any evidence to be offered by him. Therefore, I submit to this honorable court that the witness's testimony constitutes "tainted fruit of the poisonous tree," and that this witness should be dismissed and the jury instructed to disregard any of his testimony or any evidence which he may have in his possession!"

Judge Henry Charles Rosenman had known Warren for years. The old fox had been before him many times. He could not now doubt his capable application of the fruit-of-the-tree evidence. Simply stated, whatever knowledge has been gained from an illegal confession is inadmissible. The police would not have known Masters had visited the bar if he hadn't confessed to it. They wouldn't have found Cartolla, nor have learned what he knew or possessed which would connect Masters to the rape. Since the confession was inadmissible, so was evidence which came as a result of it. He turned to Donald Scott.

"What do you know about this, Mr. Scott?" he asked.

Scott stood mute, then looked at Michaels, who slowly rose to his feet.

"How did you learn about Mr. Cartolla?" Fred was asked.

"Your Honor, we commenced a complete investigation of all of the activities of this defendant. We scoured the entire area. We ... that is, inquired around the bars and all-night places, hack stands, eateries and, well, we were very thorough and must have questioned at least, that is nearly fifty persons from the time the patrolmen were sent there until three or four hours later. It was without a doubt one of the best investigative searches made by our police. . ." He ended lamely, looking for support, a nod of the head, an encouraging smile, but no. The judge asked, "And Cartolla? Where did you find him?"

"Cartolla?" he paused. "Why, we found him in his bar! The two officers went there and found him. . ."

"In my opinion, the only way you learned about this man was from this confession. Tell me, Mr. Michaels, in all, how many bars in the area did your men search? You know what I mean, how many other bars?"

"Other bars? All told?"

The judge nodded, "Yes, please."

Fred went to his papers and searched through them, found a note, read it three or four times, then looked up sharply. "Why, in actuality, the men, Officers Melo and Bernard, went right to Cartolla's bar on orders from the precinct." He dropped the papers as the judge spoke.

147

"You know the rules, Mr. Michaels," the judge chided. "The only way you learned about this bar and this man is through the defendant's confession."

"But. . ." began Fred.

"You cannot introduce this witness, or his testimony, or any evidence through him. Please take Mr. Cartolla from the stand."

"Your Honor!" Fred stopped when he realized the truth of the matter. Shrugging his shoulders helplessly, he waived his witness down, then turned to look down at his mentor, Donald Scott, who looked up at him and simply said, "It's your case, Fred."

"I would like to ask for a recess," Fred managed.

Scott helped him to the extent of walking out of the room with him.

"Put the girl on the stand. It's all you can do now. And try to bluff it."

The two passed Susan slouched in her seat, completely ignored. They walked into the hall. Not far away Masters and Warren were in gleeful conversation.

"Maybe he'll accept a plea down . . . Maybe I can get him to copout." Fred seemed to be talking to himself.

"In no way, Fred. You've had it! Warren knows it, too. Do your best with the girl and call me." He walked away—back to his office and its unfinished cases and retirement in six months.

Cartolla walked by and handed Fred the button. Fred looked at it, thought a moment, and put it in his pocket. That goddamned illegal confession could have cost him this case.

But he still had the direct and irrefutable testimony of Julia McElroy who—his men told him, was to be in court tomorrow.

148

Twelve

"I want to continue tonight to dispel some of the myths about rape, to set the record straight. Some of these myths are so commonly held that they go unexamined. People don't even realize that they believe them; they just assume that that's the way things are.

"First, let's take the myth about black men lying in wait to attack white women. This simply isn't true. Rape takes place within, rather than across racial boundaries. More blacks are convicted because they can't afford lawyers of their own. However, of those convicted, ninety percent of the blacks have raped women of their own race."

Patricia turned to face the studio audience and a new camera picked her up.

"For centuries white males have had access to black women. During that time, whites were nearly immune from the charge of rape of black women. Women and slaves were both property, to be owned and used by men in whichever ways they pleased. One may never know how many black women were raped in this country by whites.

"You are all familiar with what we call the 'Lynch Law.' A judge in the South named Lynch became famous because he permitted a black charged with rape to be hung by a mob without a trial. Those days are over. The laws are not mob-run but they are still male-oriented.

"As to the typical rapist—he is a single man, about 23 years old, who will victimize a woman of about 19.6 years old.

"The rapist can be a sadist, a psychopath who proves his sexual mastery by causing pain and inflicting violence on his victim. He bears tremendous hostility toward women, and only by hurting them can he achieve sexual release.

"On the other hand, he may not be vicious, but only insecure, and will attempt to show his virility by taking a passive woman by force.

"Dr. Menachem Amir categorized different types of rapists in *Sexual Behavior* magazine this way:

"One: 'Offenders for whom the crime is a symptom or an idiosyncratic act either psychopathological or due to special circumstances; it is devoid of direct social role significance. This type of offender is treated with most concern, but is in a minority.' This is the man we think of as the mad rapist.

"Two: 'Offenders for whom the crime is mainly a role-supportive act, usually part of a youth culture role. That is, the act is performed for the purpose of maintaining membership in a group or for sheer sexual gratification, while pathology is absent.' This would include the young men who are trying to prove their masculinity.

150

"Dr. Amir's third category includes 'the offenders for whom the crime is mainly a role-expressive act. It is performed not so much for sexual satisfaction as because of participation in the context which it occurred, for example group rape.'

"The frightening thing about these categories, and about the statistics we've come across, is that a majority of rapists seem to be trying to *prove* something to themselves, to society. They are trying to prove that they are men, that they have grown up and are ready to take on the role of superiority toward women."

Patricia leaned forward in her chair, and the camera zoomed in for a close-up.

"Something must be terribly wrong with our culture's definition of masculinity if a man has to beat a woman into submission and brutally take her—to prove that he is a man. This is Patricia Rankin, for Group One News. Next week, we're going to take a closer look at this masculinity identity problem, and at the gang rape which has become a far too common adolescent puberty rite."

After the broadcast, Patricia and Joe Fontana had their usual supper. The cafe was empty for some reason and she began expressing her personal feelings. "I like to sound off on the air about the trial I'm seeing in person, the People versus poor Susan, whom you know, I've made a friend."

". . .as well as the DA."

She glanced at Joe and smiled. "Really Joe, you guys are worse than women!"

"If you mean we're gossips, we are!"

"I would like to let the public know what goes on inside a courtroom when a woman goes to court as a rape victim. It would seem that the poor man was picked up on the street and dragged in without cause and made to stand trial for being a man, while the woman, a lewd and stupid creature who has nothing but sex and perversion on her sadistic mind, bites her own breasts for kicks and goes about picking on innocent men. You really ought to attend one of these trials some day and see how horribly we are being treated because we can't fight off sexual attack. I guess the only answer is Kung Fu or karate classes. Then, whenever we want to accept a man we'll drop our guard, both physical and mental. But if we don't, men watch out! You'll end up with more than a bitten breast.

"In fact," she summarized, "you can't look at the victim and then at the accused and confessed rapist, without drawing your own conclusion that if sex was known to this girl—as it most likely was—she surely did not ask that man to get involved with her!"

Joe took her hand and became very serious. "Patricia, I know how upset this series has made you and I must caution you once more—whether you're personally involved with that DA or not—you must be careful! You cannot get involved in a civil law suit charging us with taking a personal position in a criminal case. So cool it, despite your good ratings and the fact you are now more than ever a celebrity!"

She knew he was going on the record. The telephone call from Fred carried a more serious message.

"I can't find Julia McElroy!"

Later, at her apartment over a nightcap, he told her.

"We've had detectives trying to locate her for about two weeks. She was subpoenaed to appear tomorrow. I don't actually have to have her for corroboration with the new law, yet . . . if I did have her it would be more convincing to the jury. She saw Masters run away! She took Susan to her home, to the hospital, and to the police. She was practically in on it from the moment the rape was completed! It would be telling testimony."

"Why don't you try her doorman? They always know more than they pretend."

"We did. Her super said she packed up, kids and all. Doesn't know for where or how long. I'm going berserk!"

"We'll cool it together after the broadcast. I'll meet you at the same place."

Susan went to court alone the next day. Fred was still looking for Julia, but Susan couldn't imagine her not being there.

On the steps a man with a mike came over to Susan. Suddenly she realized they were aiming the lens of the camera at her and that a crowd had stopped and stood waiting her answer. She froze.

"We are here to get a 'people-on-the-street' reaction to a rape trial going on inside there. By any chance are you aware of it?"

Jesus! Was he kidding? She pushed at the mike, tears forming, blood rushed to her face. Then the man seemed to recognize her, mumbled something incoherent, and started backing off.

"That's her!" a woman's voice yelled from the steps beneath her. He turned and looked. "It's you? Susan Landress, the rape victim?"

Then a man was yelling at them from behind her. With her hands before her face she couldn't be sure but it sounded like Fred. "For Chrissake, leave her alone, you idiot!"

Feet pounding . . . and a man in a fight.

She didn't wait to see the outcome. Patricia Rankin's camera crew had been sent there to get her, after all the promises! She went through the crowd on the sidewalk pushing and shoving, tears blinding her, and a man shouting behind her. At the red light he caught up. His hand was on her elbow.

"Sorry about that! With all the publicity it was inevitable. I killed the film they had on you, threatened an injunction and the FCC. Chuck Reeves is a good guy. He just got overzealous."

It was Fred.

"Thanks," she managed. "I'm going home; maybe you'll get me there safely. I think I'm going to throw up."

Before Fred dropped her off at her apartment he had convinced her that Patricia had not set her up.

"As I said, the news department goes out on assignments arranged by the news director. This case has become pretty famous, what with Sturdevant Warren giving out 'bulletins,' and the national press aroused over the new rape laws and the first few cases. You must remember, you agreed to fight for all women, not just for yourself. You knew what would happen."

"But not this . . . this invasion!"

"Susan, believe me, this is only the beginning."

That night the *Daily News* ran a three-paragraph box on the *People* v. *Masters* case and stated that the attorney for the defense had won a major point by relying on the ancient "fruit of the poisoned tree" rule which forbade the use of tainted testimony from a confession which had been disallowed. "This case is fast becoming a 'landmark' with Warren, the well-known socialite, handling his first rape case. To quote him: 'I feel men have been denied justice in false charges of rape from the hands of promiscuity too long. I am happy to be defending Masters.'"

In Gstaadt, Switzerland, no one read about the case, nor could care less, except Julia McElroy, whose return home was delayed due to her impending marriage.

In New York, now dependent upon her as a witness to directly accuse Masters of having raped Susan, Fred went back to Julia's apartment and made his own inquiry.

Mail was now being forwarded, care "Dr. J. F. Fullerton, Hotel Garde, Gstaadt, Switzerland."

Then Fred spoke to the super. "Yeah, we got a letter from her. She flew to get married to this medico she was seein' here. A cell-cure guy. No quack. Had a beard. She's a nice lady. Hope it works out for her, Terry, and Barbara. Understand the doc has two of his own, Susan, I think her name is ... and Wesley ... or was it Timmy? No, that was her husband's first name..."

"Did she leave any word for me...?" It was, of course, hopeless.

"Actually she didn't let us know she was going for good. Her stuff's being shipped ... through John Benson's Moving and Storage. Does that help?"

The next morning Fred reached her by telephone.

"If you need me, I'll come back. I didn't think you people needed corroboration any more. I've read so much about it."

"What you saw and did is very necessary evidence. His rape confession was thrown out of court. We need all we can get. That means you!"

After hanging up, Fred felt relieved and told Patricia so. "I'll put Susan on and try to protect her from Sturdevant Warren. I'll get her to tell it like it happened and then I'll have her identify him."

"I don't see how a jury could not believe Susan," said Patricia. "Why would she go through all this if she hadn't really been raped. What's in it for her?"

"Susan Landress to the stand!"

"Seats! Take seats!" shouted the bailiff and watched the courtroom subside. The judge sat down and shifted about uncomfortably. The judge didn't like rape cases. Women always got the worst of it. He had sat at civil, as well as criminal rape trials. In civil suits the woman, having sued in a civil action, faced countersuits for damages if she couldn't prove rape. Now he would see this near-child to her denouement in a criminal case. In this action Masters could refuse to testify; he couldn't really do so in a civil case because the jury would draw inferences.

Rumor in the hallways had it that Michaels was going to have to put the victim on as a final witness, that Julia McElroy hadn't been found yet to put the coup de grace to Masters. The judge watched Susan carefully take her seat as idle thoughts and cliches came to mind. She was the image of wronged womanhood, tiny-boned, graceful in contrast to the hulking Masters. Her placid face indicated a childlike faith in justice for her outraged innocence. Surely that is the way rape complainants should come on, he thought. That was the way to a jury's heart. Her face was pale and set, her blue eyes set straight forward, long legs interlocked, modesty and femininity confronting the eyes upon her. Fred slowly walked toward her.

156

"Miss Landress, please tell us where you live."

Her voice was low. "At 413 East 63rd Street, New York."

"What do you do?"

"Right now?"

"Why, yes, Miss Landress. Right now."

"I work in an ad agency. I am a clerk . . . I work on a charity account. It benefits orphaned children."

"Very good, Miss Landress. Good." He paused to let her worthy and good activity distil in the minds of zealous jurors looking for immoral behavior in an attractive girl who had been raped.

"And were you in advertising on a charity account on the night of May 12 last year?"

"Oh, no sir."

"Then what was your occupation on that date?"

"I worked in another advertising agency."

"And what did you do in that advertising agency?" Fred stepped away from her and moved toward the jury, which was watching her closely. She turned to follow him.

"I was executive secretary to the owner."

"And what were your duties?"

"I took dictation, arranged his appointments, generally fielded complaints and calls from clients, that sort of thing."

"And on the night of May 12 had you begun working for that firm?"

"No. I had not. On that night I was unemployed."

"Did you leave your residence that night?"

"Yes, I did. I wanted to get some fresh air."

"And what time did you leave?"

"It was . . . about eleven o'clock."

An older lady juror smiled knowingly.

"Why did you go out at night that late?"

"I don't know. I felt like it. I'm not used to being afraid of the night."

The older juror smiled again and looked left and right. No question. This girl was a hooker.

"What kind of neighborhood do you live in? I mean is it busy at night at that hour?"

"There are restaurants and singles bars around there."

"Is the sidewalk a busy thoroughfare or is it deserted at eleven?"

"It is well-lit, crowded with young people. I felt safe, if that's what you mean."

"Yes, that's what I mean. Do you always take a walk at that hour?"

"No. Not at all. I think it was the first time. I went out that night because it was my birthday—and I was alone."

"You were born on May 12, the day of the alleged rape?" Fred hadn't been aware of that himself. What a break for sympathy.

"Yes."

"How old were you on that day, Miss Landress?"

"I was twenty-one."

"So instead of going to your lonely apartment on your birthday you sought the environment of a happy crowd?"

She looked from her lap up at him. "No. It wasn't that. I sort of . . . well, I guess I just wandered."

"And where did this lonely wandering take you?"

"I walked toward the river. I love the water. It helps me unwind."

"Miss Landress were you particularly homesick that night?"

She put her hands inside her pocketbook and extracted a tissue but didn't use it. "It was . . . my

158

birthday, sir," she smiled, "and I missed my mom and my brother Doug."

"I see. So you wandered on your birthday to the river? Why the river, Miss Landress?"

"I always go to water when I want to think. On the Coast it was the ocean. I don't know why."

"Perfectly natural. There is nothing wrong in that. Now, please tell the jury what happened to you as you wandered in complete loneliness feeling terribly homesick on your birthday all alone in New York."

"Look, Your Honor," interrupted Warren, on his feet. "This whole thing is irrelevant. Just let the witness answer where she was. We don't have to know why. The District Attorney should keep his 'perfectly natural' comments to himself."

"Will you please go on, Miss Landress, and tell us what happened that night?" Fred broke in with a frown at Warren.

"I reached the river—it was dark but I saw a little park. It seemed like a nice place to sit and think."

"And you went in?"

"Yes."

"Miss Landress, how long had you lived in New York City?"

"Before that night?"

"Yes, before the night in question."

"I had just gotten here. About three days."

"And it never occurred to you that prowlers or muggers or ... rapists ... could be about in dark parks at that hour?"

"It never occurred to me at all. I didn't think about them."

"So you went into the park unaware of danger, having come from a seacoast city in California?"

"Yes."

"Do people walk about in that city at night?"

"On the beach, in the parks, yes."

"What happened that night?"

"A man raped me."

Warren was up shouting. "Your Honor, she is arriving at a legal conclusion! Please instruct the witness to answer only in terms of fact, not her fantasies."

Fred flashed back. "This is no fantasy. What I will develop with my witness is a brutal attack which no girl could fantasize . . . no one, let alone Miss Susan Landress."

The judge said, "Please, gentlemen, desist. Let her go on with her own story in her own words. Please, Miss Landress, continue."

Susan recoiled. The shouting over her—the yelling between the two lawyers unnerved her.

"Miss Landress?" Fred was saying, "do you hear me?"

(Yes, I hear you and I see you and all the other leering men in this room, and I know what you are thinking about me. I know you look at me as if I had lured this innocent man into that park and made him attack me. I see it in your eyes as they undress me, in your ears as you listen to me, and in your guts as you imagine being with me.)

"Miss Landress," Michaels was saying. "Please! Don't you hear me? I want you to describe what it was like that night . . . just like it happened."

(Yes, I hear you and I will tell you what it was like that night.) She started talking, rapidly as if in a dream and in a monotone, her eyes dead and a film began unreeling before her eyes as a young woman walked alone in a park, and a husky man ran at her and grabbed her by the throat.

"He had me by the throat before I knew what was

160

happening. He bent me back and tripped me. I fell down. I thought I had sprained an ankle. He was very strong. I tore at his face with my nails. But he held my arms. His forearm was pressed down against my neck cutting off my wind. Then while I took a breath he leapt up over me and he ... and he ... unzipped his trousers ...

"Then he threw himself on top of me. This time he worked on my blazer, tore it off, and ripped at my blouse. But I fought for my life. He ripped off the shorts. He was like an animal. He bit me like an animal. Every time I hit him with my one free hand, he hit me hard on the face with his fist over and over and over. Then, after he had done that, he reached down. I could feel his hand.

"I knew what was going to happen but I was afraid for my life. He kept telling me what he was doing and what he was going to do next and it was horrible. He said ... he said if I didn't let him he would strangle me. I was almost unconscious when he did it; it was like a knife! I fought but I didn't want to die. I thought ... I wondered why not just let him ... but I didn't stop fighting. I scratched at his back, but he paid no attention. I had one arm free but I couldn't use it. He was on top of me, with his legs between mine and his chest against mine. What could I do? What could I do? Oh, God, I tried! I tried to scream. I couldn't even whisper with his arm across my throat and his other arm pinning me down and holding me. I tried hard not to let him. . ."

She had her hands at her eyes but she went on. Fred watched the stenographer take it all down. The jury stared at her. "I didn't want to be raped. I fought back. Then after he pulled away from me, I couldn't move. I was like dead and he stood up. I couldn't

161

move. I was numb and gasping to breathe. Then he flopped me over saying what he was going to do next and I tried to move away on my hands and knees but he fell on me . . . on my back and he . . . They call it 'sodomy.' He tore into me. I couldn't believe it was happening. Oh, God, I prayed. I asked for help . . . I tried to scream. But he held me around the throat and after he was through with me he pushed my face into the dirt cursing and yelling at me. I heard him running away and then someone came to help me. . ." Susan's head was in her hands and she was sobbing.

"Miss Landress," asked Fred gently, "please tell the jury. Do you see the man who assaulted you in this courtroom?"

In the silence, she raised her head, then pointed. Her finger leveled at Guy Masters. "That is the man who raped me. That is him."

Before anyone could speak Fred said, "Let the record show that the witness, Susan Landress, is pointing at the defendant, Guy Masters."

Warren was clearly upset. He stood for a moment shaking his head and looking from Susan to Fred.

"Your Honor, I object." he started. "I object to histrionics, emotional outbursts, and dramatic recitations of what she says took place."

The judge shook his head. "Be seated, sir. Your objections are overruled!"

"Miss Landress," continued Fred, "are you absolutely certain that the man who raped you is Guy Masters, without a shadow of a doubt?"

"That man raped me. It was him! He did it! He should be in jail now!"

"Objection!" shouted Warren. "The witness is going too far. She has testified that she went through a trying experience and it must be difficult for her to report it ... but there is really no need to excite the jury with dramatics and collapsing witnesses." Susan was obviously near collapse, gripping the arms of her chair tightly to maintain control, to stop shaking.

"Your Honor," said Fred, "she has stated what happened to her in her own words as she recalls it. Let the record stand."

"In my objection, sir, I include reference to the phantom breast bite, for one thing."

Warren would not sit down. "Your Honor, there is no evidence that she more than fantasized that a man bit her breast. I object to it, Your Honor ... particularly, sir ... particularly when no evidence has been entered to prove the bite, the brutalized breast, or even a small cut, bruise, abrasion, or mark. Sir, the only thing for us to do is to demand that the witness take off her dress, right now, and expose the area where she states my client bit her, and let us see with our own eyes—let the people and the jury and the judge see just what evidence there is of it. I ask you to instruct her to bare her breast!"

Susan gasped, drew her hands protectively to her breasts, and screamed, the cry of a wounded animal, "No ... no ... no ... You can't..."

The courtroom was in an immediate uproar. Jury members leaned forward. The judge pounded. The police walked up and down the aisle and the two lawyers were before the judge shouting and gesturing.

When the room had quieted down, the judge denied Warren's request and asked Fred whether he had any further questions.

With his answer that he would withdraw pending arrival of another witness, Susan stepped down from the stand and he and the judge set the time to reconvene on Monday. The clerk led her back to Michaels, who put his arm around her.

"You were great. I'm sorry for what you went through. Tomorrow Warren will really tear into you. Try to get some sleep."

He saw that she was weeping as he helped her into a taxi. And he saw that they were not the tears of a child, quick to come and quick to disappear. They were the tears of a woman in despair, a woman who had lost something and had given up hope of ever getting it back.

"Don't worry," he told her. "Julia McElroy will be here. She's flying in. We'll put Masters away. You are very brave."

It was 4:00 P.M. by the time Fred could see Scott, who was in his office calling the airport again. "Why doesn't someone check the goddamn passenger list? Well, for God's sake hurry. Time has run out."

Fred sat opposite him waiting, a dejected look on his face. "For Chrissake, now where the hell is Julia McElroy?"

Scott was waiting for word, his hand over the mouthpiece. "You're damned lucky for a long weekend ahead. Warren must figure you planned to stall until we get our prize witness in court. It does buy us time!" His angry face took on an eager look as he pressed his ear to the receiver, "Yes? Yes? Son of a bitch!" He paused. "Check passports ... immigration. Maybe she used another name with the airline. Her name is Julia Morrow McElroy."

A clerk opened his office door. "May I interrupt?" He held an envelope. Fred motioned him to silence. "Quiet!"

"But . . . but . . . "

Scott had his ear jammed to the phone, saw the yellow envelope in the clerk's hand, and waved him in. Resting the telephone against his shoulder, he tore open the envelope. A voice spoke to him but he didn't hear it. He was reading the cable. Slowly he dropped it. "Never mind, Frank, we just got a cable from her. 'SORRY CAN'T MAKE IT. BOBBY DOWN WITH THE MEASLES.' Did you hear that, for Chrissake? Someone named Bobby is down with the measles and Masters gets away with rape!"

After twenty-eight years of dedicated service, maintaining his aplomb and composure, D. P. Scott had finally blown up. He was yelling at the world at the top of his lungs. "Some goddamned silly kid has the friggin' measles and we lose an important witness against a son of a bitch who destroyed a human being. I just can't believe this is happening to me!"

"To you!" said Fred in disgust, his hand running violently through his hair. "Jesus Christ, D.P., there is a girl involved!"

"Well, why did she get involved in the first place?"

Fred walked out and slammed the door.

Thirteen

On Sunday, Susan said she had time to meet with Patricia and they agreed on one o'clock at the Sherry Netherlands. After a drink and a green salad, they walked out into the sun of Central Park, passed the bookmobiles, the marimba-steel bands, and walked down the mall. On either side, the benches were lined with sunbathers, old couples, and children. At the zoo, they watched the sea lions, threw some peanuts into the cages, and watched the elephants.

"You know," said Patricia, "the mammoths of the world hide when they have sex. Both the whale and the elephant. The whale deep down under water; the elephant into the depth of the jungle. No one has ever seen them mate in their natural habitat."

They sat on the grass and Susan unburdened herself.

"You know, Patricia, you are doing just fine with my case. It's simply outstanding. I mean what you're doing for womankind. But not for me personally. I mean it's great that you're telling women that 'a rapist is trying to prove his masculinity.' But what about the victim? What about me? It doesn't mean a damn thing to me if 'a rapist is a sadist who bears a tremendous hostility to women and who is obsessed with a need for mastery through sexual conquest.' So what? What does it matter why he did it? He ruined my life.

"Some weirdo hit on me, when I was minding my own business. I'm like someone who's been mowèd down by a tornado and the whole world is sorry and they send supplies and food and the Red Cross. But that's not what I need. I need a place to live in.

"That's what Masters took away from me—my body. He didn't steal my purse or my coat or my television set. He stole my body, he ripped it up and used it and ruined it forever. . .for me. . .for any other man I want to give it to. I have to live in this body for the rest of my life. And there is no way I can get it clean again."

Susan was angrier than Patricia had ever seen her. Something was different. From being a small, frightened, wounded girl, Susan Landress had become an angry woman, and as she spoke her voice took on a rasping rage, rather than the whimper of pain.

"That son of a bitch ought to be beaten up by a bunch of men—and women—and castrated. I oughta be able to tie him up and cut his bloody balls off, slice him up. Ruin him."

Susan was scared of her own emotions; she hadn't known how much hate she had for that man, maybe now for all men.

"Ruin him. . .ruin. . ." she said over and over, her

anger now turning to frustration as she realized the impossibility of revenge. She sobbed as she continued, more calmly now, pleading for understanding.

"It's just so awful, Patricia. Every time I undress I see myself as he saw me. My body no longer seems like a way to pleasure—it's pain. And the awful thing is, that's not the worst of it. He didn't just steal my body, Patricia, that man killed my soul. He didn't just rape my body, he found the most personal, private part of my being, of my mind, and bloodied it all up.

"See. . .I'm not the same person I was before. I can never go back."

Patricia put her arm around Susan, a gesture which would have usually been very difficult. "I know, Susan, I know," she said. "At least I can understand what you're telling me. And what can I say? I'm sorry? God, yes, I'm sorry. Something is really fucked up in this world, something's gone wrong, gone mad. All I can say is that you've got to put it behind you. You've got to go on. You're very young, you're bright, you're pretty. Maybe when Fred gets that guy put away you'll feel better.

"If it gives you any strength, honey, just remember that what you're doing you're doing for me and every other woman in this country. I know it's horrible, but without your sacrifice, and the other women who sacrifice to take these men to court, rapists would never be convicted."

"I *was* a sacrifice," said Susan.

That evening back at her apartment, Susan sat down to write a long, newsy letter to Dougie. But she didn't get very far. What was there to write about? She wasn't working, she had to go to trial every day. She wasn't dating, no way was she going to go out alone and try to meet men. She wasn't meeting exciting, interesting people. The only ones she knew besides Anne were those connected with the trial, and she couldn't write to him about that.

She sat at the kitchen table a long time, doodling on the stationery, writing the words over and over again: rape, RAPE VICTIM, RAPE VICTIM, RAPE VICTIM.

In court the next day, Fred could see that Susan was withdrawing from her surroundings. She seemed almost comatose, vaguely disoriented.

Warren started banging away. Standing arrogantly before her like a Moses who had things to say to a delinquent sinner, he asked, "Miss Landress, prior to your visit to the park on the evening of May 12, had you had sexual intercourse?"

She looked up at him and stared.

"Please answer me, Miss Landress. Had you engaged in sexual intercourse prior to the walk you took in the park?"

She said, "No."

"When was the last time prior to that walk that you had sexual intercourse?"

Michaels objected. The judge allowed it.

Susan looked at the judge. "Do I have to answer that?"

"Please, Miss Landress, let him develop his point."

She looked up at the ceiling, ignoring the people leaning forward in their seats. "About two weeks prior to that "

"I see," said Moses.

"And," he went on, "you take the Pill?"

She nodded.

"What?"

"Yes, I do."

"Why?"

"Objection!" said Fred. "Irrelevant."

"I am trying to establish something about the character of the complainant, Your Honor. Her charge of rape must be based on knowledge. My next question will show you what I mean."

"Next question."

"Miss Landress, can you tell the Court about your first—your very first—sexual experience."

"Objection!" exclaimed Fred. Susan withered.

"I merely wish to ascertain whether the experience in the park as described by Miss Landress was her first."

"Then so ask, Mr. Warren," said the judge.

"Miss Landress, do you know what. . .sexual intercourse is?" he said with a bright smile.

"Yes, I do," she said. How she hated this man.

"What is sexual intercourse, Miss Landress?"

"Why, it's . . . it is . . . Please, do I have to answer? You know what it is. What are you trying to get me to say?"

"I'm not trying to get you to say anything, Miss Landress. Just what, in your opinion, is normal sexual intercourse?"

"Your Honor," interrupted Fred. "I think this question is absolutely and entirely irrelevant."

"I will rephrase it again if it will suit you, sir. Now please, Miss Landress, does penetration have anything to do with sexual intercourse? Do you know what I mean by penetration?"

"Penetration?"

"Yes, penetration."

"That's when a man puts his . . . er. . ."

"That's right." He seemed to be trying to make it easier for her. "Do you think a man and a woman can have sexual intercourse without penetration?"

"I guess not."

"You guess not! Can a woman use something else? Say a candle, and have normal sexual intercourse with a man?"

"No."

"Then you agree that penetration of the man's penis into her vagina is necessary for normal sexual relationships?"

"Yes."

"How many times a year do you suppose you have engaged in the act of sexual intercourse?"

"Me?"

"You."

"I don't see the relevance of this," objected Fred.

But Warren ignored the interruption. "Did you have sexual relationships with your husband, a returned war veteran from Viet Nam, a hero?"

She lost all sense of time or place. What was happening to her? He was asking her too many intimate things. Why did they let him continue? What did that have to do with her charge of rape against Guy Masters?

"I ask you again! Did you have sexual intercourse with your husband, a Green Beret, veteran of Viet Nam with an honorable discharge?"

"Yes."

"Are you aware that a man cannot rape his own wife? Are you aware that under law a man cannot, absolutely cannot, rape his own wife?"

"I don't know. . ."

"Well, it's true. Now Miss Landress, after your marriage to this war hero did you go to Dallas from the wedding?"

She nodded.

"Isn't it a fact that on the wedding night, the first night of your honeymoon, when a man might expect to consummate his wedding, you ran away from him screaming and crying? Is that not a fact?"

"Objection! He is leading the witness."

"Your Honor, I merely wish to prod the witness, who seems unwilling to speak."

"This is cross-examination and I will permit him some latitude. . ." The judge asked her kindly, "Please tell us about the circumstances."

"I ran away when he told me that he was married to someone else. . .that he was a bigamist."

Warren backed off suddenly. Michaels got to his feet. The judge peered over and looked at her.

"Are you saying, Miss Landress, that your husband committed bigamy when he married you?"

"Yes, Your Honor. I ran away from him that night. There is an annulment suit being filed now."

Fred began making notes. He'd have to ask her later why she hadn't told him about her husband; or the bigamy. Jesus, Patricia should be here! Not those scribbling reporters. It would be shot out to the papers in Santa Monica and despite her efforts to keep her rape case from her family, it would be in the local papers.

"Miss Landress," began Warren now fully recovered, "is it true that from experiences such as that —that you feel men—men in general are rough on women?"

"Rough? What do you mean?"

"Yes or no."

"No."

"Aren't they a little too brutal on feminine feelings?"

She didn't answer.

"Objection!" shouted Fred from his feet.

"Miss Landress, isn't it true that men are really a little too brutal for you?"

172

"Objection!"

". . .and that you have now turned to the opposite sex, your own sex—women?"

"No!" she cried, suddenly alert.

"Isn't it true that men are rough with your body, that they hurt you and are savage, and that you have now turned to women?"

"Objection. This is entirely irrelevant."

"I will prove that it has a bearing on her sexual attitudes and that they have a great bearing on her charge of rape against my client."

"Sustained. Please strike the question and move on."

"Miss Landress," started Warren, "is it not true that you are now engaged in a lesbian affair?"

"My God!" she cried, her hands before her face.

"I object to this line of questioning, Your Honor," said Fred. "I find it highly irrelevant."

"Your Honor, I will show that it is very relevant and in detail. I am going to show that her lesbian activities are a result of an attitude about all men, my client included, and that she now plays the active role in a lesbian relationship, that she is totally disgusted by any man attempting to show the slightest affection, and is unstable in her relationships with all men. I believe it furnishes the motive for her accusations against my client. It takes the form of fantasies such as those so graphically described by her as occurring on the night of her birthday. They indicate great loneliness and hunger for human, loving companionship. It explains why she believed she was having intercourse with a man."

"Proceed, Mr. Warren."

"Miss Landress, do you now live with another woman?"

Susan seemed surprised at the question. "Why, sure." She answered. What did Anne have to do with her charge of rape against Guy Masters?

"Miss Landress," asked Warren, "are you aware of your roommate's arrest record? Do you know how many times she has been involved in disturbances at homosexual bars?"

Susan stared at him in disbelief.

"Do you have a homosexual relationship with your roommate?"

Susan broke into tears. "No," she finally answered. "I have never done what you said."

"Miss Landress," asked the judge, in a low voice, but loud enough for the jury to hear, "Are you a lesbian?"

She couldn't answer such a question. What was happening here? Circumstantial evidence. She had suspected that Anne preferred women, but she had never made a pass. How could Warren bring this up? What evidence, what right did he have? What did it matter anyway?

The judge leaned toward her waiting.

"God, no! Your Honor!"

She said it with such distaste it didn't seem possible the judge or any member of the jury could disbelieve her.

But Warren sneered—then came forward again, his manner and tone making it clear he was dealing with a liar.

"We'll get back to this later. Now one further question which I hope to get a straight answer about this time. Miss Landress, would you call yourself an exhibitionist?"

Again Fred shouted, "Objection! Highly irrelevant."

174

"I think his question is relevant as to the issue of consent and as to invitation in a rape case," the judge said. "She is instructed to answer the question." He turned to her and asked her to do her best. "You may answer 'Yes' or 'No.'"

Susan answered, "Of course not."

Warren snickered visibly, walked slowly to his table and selected a large brown envelope and returned to stand before her. Then, slowly and dramatically, he withdrew from it a large, ten-by-twelve glossy photograph and held it up before her so that she and only she could see it. "Is this photograph of you, Miss Landress?"

"Just one minute, Your Honor. I want to see them. I have a right to see evidence before it is entered in the record."

Warren slowly handed them over. After a brief examination, Fred said, "I object on the grounds these are totally irrelevant. They prove nothing!"

"Perhaps she doesn't know what an exhibitionist is? Do you, Miss Landress?"

She nodded, "Someone who. . ."

"May I make it easy? The dictionary definition is the act of flaunting oneself in order to attract attention. . .and in its sexual context, the exposure of sexual organs in public. The latter is a psychological problem and one which, in our present day of immoral exposure of all parts of the body in public bars and in motion pictures, is considered normal. However. . ."

"What has this to do with her charge of rape?" Fred tried to reason with the judge, shrugging his shoulders and appealing for help. "I object."

"Your Honor, this photograph, indeed all of these pictures here, are not ordinary photographs. They are

175

of the complainant, Susan Landress, in very salacious, sexual, undressed poses intended to arouse.
They do arouse." He held them tightly in his hands,
as if they might be torn from him.

"You may answer the question, Miss Landress. The
stenographer will please repeat it." The judge leaned
back with a smile. This was just another rape case,
but Warren could always be counted upon to make
his defenses interesting. He would go far in rape
defense.

The defense attorney handed her the photographs.
She reached for them and they fell, scattering before
her. Slowly he bent and gathered them while necks
craned.

They were of her alright! There she was all oily and
smooth, dancing around in that tiny bikini, lips
parted, legs spread, eyes glassy. She was horrified,
embarrassed. She hadn't realized how vulnerable
she'd been before that camera, how pornographic
those suntan photos would look in court. But whoever
thought they would be in court—that she would be
here?

"Is that you?" the loud voice of Warren cut in. "I
ask you Miss Landress—are those pictures of you—
yes or no?"

"They were taken when. . ."

"Your Honor," he interrupted. "Please instruct the
witness."

"Yes."

He turned back toward her. "What did you say?"

"I said yes, they are of me, but they were taken
when. . ."

"Thank you. That is all!"

"And this picture, Miss Landress." He held up

another which he had removed from the envelope, showing Mike Rose's hand rubbing oil between her breasts. He had set up the camera, stepped away and it had gone off automatically! Good God! Why crucify her?

"Yes, yes, yes. . .they are all of me!" she burst out.

"I enter into evidence these fourteen photographs taken of Miss Landress. . ." Warren began, looking at the judge and then at the jury, "by the former boss of this complainant, Mr. Michael Rose, for whom she posed in his studio in the act of sexual foreplay and state that she is undoubtedly an exhibitionist who might tantalize any man who crosses her path as she tantalized Mr. Rose." The double meaning was not lost.

It was all wrong, they didn't understand. Sobbing again, her hands gesturing wildly, Susan stood up. "But I was unaware. . .I was not told. I didn't know. . .I didn't know!"

But no one listened to her. They were all craning their necks, pushing and holding others back. The judge reached for the photos. The clerk beat him to them. He started looking. His face got redder. The judge leaned forward. The clerk marked them carefully and slowly. Then with regret he handed them to the judge above him. The judge began a careful examination of the latest evidence.

"With your permission," interrupted Warren, "I would like the jury to have them and to make a complete inspection of the evidence." The judge didn't hear him. . .just kept turning from one photo to the next. Then he looked up suddenly with a sort of double take, saw the entire room was watching him, flushed, and handed them to the attorney.

"Thank you," said Warren and gave them to the jury foreman.

The photos were reluctantly surrendered from juror to juror, until they were all completely absorbed in the pornographic display. Here one grabbed. There another held on. Finally, after twenty minutes, they were finished and handed the prints back.

Susan was still in shock. She was mortified. Warren stood before her.

"Now Miss Landress, I want to ask you another question. At any time in your life have you ever been convicted of a crime?"

"No."

"Never? Not even one teenie-weenie one, once?"

"No." She sounded indignant.

"I would like, Your Honor, to offer into evidence a certified transcript of a conviction issued out of the Criminal Court of Pleas in Santa Monica, California, County of Los Angeles, dated four years ago, in which it shows the witness to have been convicted of the crime of larceny."

"Objection!" challenged Fred.

"You know the law is very clear on this, Mr. Michaels," reminded the judge. "The document is certified and may be used for the purpose of impeaching this witness." He reached for the document and examined it, while nodding at what he read.

"Miss Landress," asked Warren, "I show you this certified document and ask you whether it refreshes your memory and recollection as to your prior criminal record." He took it from the judge and handed it to the clerk for entry. Then he handed her the paper. "Why," she said, "I guess when I was a kid, like a lot of others in the neighborhood, we snitched a few things from Haley's Department Store on Fourth and Santa Monica. It was only five dollars worth of. . ."

"Thank you, that is all." He turned his back on her. Looking at the jury he said, "Imagine! Only five dollars worth! She was convicted of larceny. The judge didn't think she was 'only a kid.'

"Now Miss Landress, did you ever bite your own breast?"

"Objection!" Fred was on his feet, fuming, "Haven't we had enough of this?"

"I'll rephrase the question. Was it Mike Rose who bit your breast?"

"No."

"Then who did? Was it Anne Treadwell?"

"No. It was him!" She pointed to Guy Masters.

"Did you ever exhibit this bitten breast to anyone?"

"To the doctor at the hospital."

"Dr. Hugh Margate?"

"If that's his name."

"When you were examined by this doctor, did he go over you completely?"

"Go over me? Yes. That . . . well."

"Well did you point out the wound on your breast?"

"I don't recall. It was very embarrassing. . .the whole thing. . .lying there with. . ."

"Never mind the details. Now answer me. If you had been severely bitten, why didn't you call his attention to it and show him your breast?"

She didn't answer. He went on. "Which breast was it, the right?"

She paused before answering. "Why no. It was the left." Her hand went unconsciously to it. The gesture was very convincing. He shot a question at her quickly.

"When you stood in the dark of the park that night, you had just come in from a well-lighted street?"

"Yes, I guess so. I think it was well lighted. I don't remember."

"I have here a Lumin's Test showing that the light on the sidewalk around the park is sufficient to read a newspaper like the *Daily News* held at a normal distance from the eyes." He held up a sheet of paper. "I enter this in evidence as proof that the area around the park is well lighted."

It was accepted.

"Now inside the park, Miss Landress, when you first entered it, how far was this man whom you say attacked you?"

"Twenty feet."

"Can you see things that far away in normal daylight?"

"I would think so."

"Miss Landress, do you wear contact lenses or any variety of visual aid whether for reading or for seeing things at a distance?"

"Oh, my God!" she cried. Now they were trying to tell her that he wasn't there in the park that night—that she couldn't see him anyway, and that she was there to entice—as an exhibitionist. What was happening here in court? She started to choke and her face grew rosy with the sudden rush of blood. Was everyone here mad? Oh, God!

Fred jumped to his feet. The judge looked at the police officer standing near her. The woman rushed behind her and began slapping her back.

Susan didn't hear him. The judge was saying, "This court is dismissed until Monday morning at ten A.M." Then he leaned solicitiously toward Susan. "Are you alright?"

180

But Susan was being helped down by the police-woman into Fred's arms. She was helped out of the courtroom. Why hadn't she just packed up and gone home. She had suffered hell in New York; life with her friends on the Coast would have been ten thousand times better than sitting here and being accused of this!

Fourteen

The Porsche 914 moved into line. The ferry was in port at Wood's Hole. It would take forty-five minutes to reach the island across the Vineyard Sound. Patricia loosened the seat belt, stepped out, and breathed the salt air.

"Board! Move into line, there! Passengers please hold their own tickets!" Seated in his car, they moved slowly up the ferry bridge into the hold of the boat, then stepped out and went on deck.

Standing next to a lifeboat, Fred pointed out the distant grey shoreline of the island. "It's on the other side. There's a wide beach, surf, and a lagoon with sixty swan, some mallards, and it's surrounded by tall salt grass. My place is there."

She hugged his arm. She would stay at an inn. The thing between them was happening, but nicely . . . with no rush. They both instinctively wanted it to be that way, to know one another well. "Not to get hurt again," she had said. He had nodded. "Never!"

After docking, they drove past the A&P, turned left and went up-island to the turnoff to Katama Plains, through the woods, past the cinder block factory, the light company, and into Edgartown.

"We turn at the cannon." He drove slowly, unlike at the high speeds he had used on the New England Thruway and Route 6A to Wood's Hole. The smell of hot bay leaves, of scrub pine, and the sea greeted them as they turned at Pease Point Way toward the lagoon road, past the old airport, and followed the grey fence posts to his camp.

Thirty minutes later they were walking hand in hand down the wide beach. Rough surf pounded up to their feet. Sandpipers escaped just in time, as if the water would damage their delicate feet while they raced like scissors after sand bugs.

"It must have been like this for Susan," she said. "I can just feel the need to undress, to run naked along here—feel the sun and wind on my body—and not to fear anything, ever!"

"Nudity is freedom ... but I'm afraid even here, where it seems deserted, it would be considered a sin to be seen that way."

"You know, Dr. Menninger says that our concept of sexual sin, and the moral values instilled in us for generations, are changing," she said. "Premarital sexual activity doesn't make a sinner out of a girl who thinks less about her body than a wild horse or a seal leaping in the waves. For centuries the mothers and fathers of the Susans were identifying 'being good' with restraint, suppression, and the denial of the body—and of sex. One can't 'gallivant around' nude. My heavens!"

"I can't change the law about nudity any more than I can about sexual misconduct," he said as he stopped, picked up a bottle, and added, "I suppose there's a genii I could let out of this Seven Up, who'd handle the matter for me." He threw it up high on the sand dunes. "I'd rather he did, than the lawmakers."

". . .and any sexual awareness in women, up to about Masters and Johnson, was *a priori* evidence of her predilection for passionate indulgence. Of course there is good and bad in sex. Like that which destroys or annihilates the personality and moral character of the participant."

"Look at that gull! I wonder if he's Jonathan? Gee, Patricia, this is heavy stuff for us—all because you want to run nude down this beach?"

As if breaking away from something which had once tied her down, she ran ahead of him. He watched her in admiration, legs flying, hair catching the salt spray, her body moving gracefully.

There is a love which breaks the heart, he thought. And she could break mine—I know she could. But she'll be loyal. She's too whole, too precious to play with. I must move slowly, but with purpose.

Patricia came running back into his open arms, as if in answer.

Later, in her inn studio suite, open to the night and the stars, they sat over a good-night Scotch.

"I've brought some tapes I must edit. Help me."

"What's our subject? Something romantic to suit that full moon?" he asked, admiring her long, plaid wool skirt and soft blue sweater. She seemed so cozy, so homey, he wanted to. . .

"The rapist. Who is he?"

He sank back in his chair. "I can't think of anything I'd rather think about, with you looking so seductive. You'd better be more the analytical TV news gatherer, and less the woman, or you'll. . ."

"He could be the boy next door," the tape began. "An Eagle Scout, a choir boy, a hostile member of a street gang."

She snapped it off. "Too long?"

"Perfect. Short and pointed."

"Your son," the tape went on, "with his peers."

She snapped it off. "I'm changing peers to friends."

"No wonder TV is rated at the seven-year-old intellectual level. Use peers."

"Your son," the tape repeated. Then she spoke into the mike. . . "with his friends." She turned it off— then on again, 'Let's find a girl,' says the group leader. Your son doesn't have the guts to say 'no' and challenge him. Result: most rapes in one major city surveyed turned out to be by adolescents. It reflects the subculture in which they live. Violence and aggressiveness rule.

"I met a European who had watched her father shot, her mother raped, and her daughter torn apart by vicious soldiers, the enemy, after World War II. Those rapists were, in a sense, taking what they thought belonged to them. For rape is considered permissible as a spoil of war. The FBI doesn't define the rapist, only the rate of increase in which he operates, which gives boys from fifteen to nineteen, and older men from twenty to twenty-four, a kind of illegal permission to join in the rise of rape in this country.

"It's as if the government was saying, 'There are more people smoking, taking drugs, and drinking than ever before.' It's a signal to the young to ape their elders. So why not rape?"

He held up his hand. She flipped it to "Off."

"Why don't you differentiate between social groups? Even though I'm rather new at it, cases I handle would have to be judged according to the social background of the victim and the accused."

"I'm coming to that. I say in here that aggression being more commonplace between those in the lower and poor classes, violent acts are frequent—including forcible sex or rape. The men are exploitative of women."

"I went on a case once to Harlem where five Puerto Rican children slept in the same room with their parents who didn't conceal their bedtime activities. I was shocked. In a child's eyes, sexual intercourse can appear to be an act of violence or physical attack, and therefore frightening."

"I've got just a little more ... random stuff. Listen to it and comment, if you care." She stamped out her cigarette. He stood up, walked over to the open door, looked out at the sky. The surf was pounding on the other side of the dunes.

"A rapist is a man whose inhibitions and social controls have broken down ... and we can't forgive him for that because he is as dangerous as a killer. Group rape is likely, however, to be more dangerous to a victim than a single rapist. First, group rapists are more likely to threaten her life—to hold her with a knife or gun—to strangle her, and to literally destroy her body. In a British survey, twenty-five percent of the rapes during a recent period were committed by groups. The victim is liable to 'flip out,' have serious mental and emotional traumas as a result, because she is being 'used' by a lot of men, as compared to a single assailant."

He interrupted. "You mean she can adjust to having turned one guy on—as a kind of surrogate lover? But that to her, gang rape by ten men is using her as a depersonalized body, an available convenience?"

186

"Yes. It's the answer to the proposition their leader posed in the beginning of their search. 'Let's find us a girl.'"

"I could never go along with that," he said quietly, "even with lining up and waiting for my turn with a prostitute. Love or sexual love is too private for me. It's never just lust."

She laughed. "You Libras. You're too sensitive. If you had been denied a woman for a long time, and you couldn't really help it, you would."

He walked back in and stood before her, a gangly kid defending himself. "Listen, teacher! I'm a guy who loves women, all females, and I love the beauty of their minds, their peculiar and delightful reasonings, and their soft and gentle hands, and their warm bodies . . . but not to share. I would want mine to be mine!"

". . . Until you tired of her or she's grown old, mean, fat, and wrinkled? Anyway, how can someone be yours?"

"Mine wouldn't let that happen. Women cheat the man with the scythe now. Father Time is being turned back by cell rejuvenation in the mountains of Switzerland. As to anyone being mine . . . I agree we are all created free and equal, even women. . ."

"Ha!" She stood up and started to swing, but he ducked and went on.

"But I have a secret belief about freedom when it comes to the equality of the sexes."

She held her fist at his nose and made a grim face. He almost grabbed her, but continued. He wanted to make his point, first. Then she'd know who he was.

"I don't think a woman should belong to a man—a lover or husband. If he—or she—lets that happen, it destroys the very thing which charmed him, which made her so appealing to him. Once she is a slave, she's simply obeying a male-created law as to his supposed rights . . . nuptial rights! And now, there's a whole new bag of misinformation and laws to suit!"

"Feminists have a viewpoint about that!" She came closer to him. "It's called a woman's nuptial right."

Pretending to be ignorant of what she meant he asked, "And what is a woman's nuptial right?"

"That the man not turn out to be impotent, the first night or ever. If it comes down to that, there should be a law: Impotence One, calling for divorce; Impotence Two, calling for separation, and so forth."

She took his hand. He said, "Maybe the man isn't ready to accept his role as the aggressor; maybe she turns him off by being too passive; ready, willing, and waiting for him to be able."

"Rubbish!" she said. "A man can get an annulment if the woman refuses what is called 'his rights.' Who said she shouldn't have rights, too?"

"Rape draws the line. One side involves the impotent male; the other, the rapist, who is the overacting male. It's a male role to attack, to overpower the adversary. The woman. . ."

Patricia interrupted: ". . .is taught all her life to cover up, to retreat, to be modest, not to arouse, unless she wants the ultimate contact. She's told to be submissive, not permissive, to be modest not enticing, and to scream, 'Hands off! You lout! Marry me or go to the dungeon!' Then the man on the white horse, the legal reinforcement, rushes in and says, 'Foul! you desecrated womanhood.'"

"And misused her beautiful body?"

"It's all we're supposed to have. Although I'll accept any other credit you are willing to accord me."

He tried to interrupt the flow of words, but she stopped him, took his hand, and held it. "Fred, you know once a woman begins to understand what's behind the violence of rape—to grapple with the psychology of it and the bestiality—she gets pretty damned disgusted. . ."

"With all men?"

"Well she could, really. Unless her guy is a lot different. But she might also get a reaction about her guy's er . . . well, manhood."

"His maleness . . . his drive, the urgency of his sex?"

"Not really. A woman in love with a man expects that. But it's the foul play she hates. She is born into a female life with a role to play, out of which she is only now emerging into a kind of. . ."

"If you say 'sisterhood' I'll scream!"

"Sisterhood. . ." He held both her hands and she looked into his eyes as she continued. "I mean that so-called budding sisterhood between women, which you guys find funny because after all, we are second class at best. Why would we want to hang together? If it's so funny, why are you worried?" She tried to pull away. What was this? Fred was being dominating all of a sudden, relying on his strength to win an argument. He must be kidding.

Instead he let go.

"I don't find it funny—and don't equate me with the phallic chauvinist tribe. I believe women are superior to men. First, they are designed better physically, capable of a longer life. Second, they have sensitivities men don't, and they have a spiritual side that no man can penetrate no matter how many times he rapes her."

She stood up. "Yah, and men, on the other hand, just happen to be stronger, more logical, and naturally aggressive?"

He stood next to her. "Aw, come on. You know

we're not going to solve this problem tonight. Maybe it's unnatural, Patricia, or maybe it's natural, but I'm beginning to feel kind of aggressive. I feel like a man —don't you feel like a woman?"

He took her in his arms. Then they made love and she answered him. "Yes, Fred, I feel like a woman."

To Susan all the nights seemed alike. She had stopped all outside activities since the trial began. The ad agency job was put on ice because of all the publicity, but her boss there had said he understood and not to worry: "There is always a job here for you."

While alone, she thought a lot about the attitudes of people she'd met. From the day the call to police headquarters had elicited disbelief from the desk sergeant, to the night the cops had come at her call when she believed Masters was prowling outside her door. "Voyeurs don't rape!" the sergeant had said, trying to calm her down. "Go to bed and relax."

After he had posted a cop at her door with an order to "Stay awhile until she gets to sleep," he had gone with open siren and flashing light spelling out his retreat.

She had slammed and locked the door. Three locks. Certain.

She had heard her tormentor's laugh. The kind a man makes when his quarry doesn't know what she is missing. Then his retreating steps. A loud banging of elevator doors and down he went.

Protect her indeed!

After seeing Humphrey Bogart in an old flick made thirty years ago in which he seemed so old and so cool, she walked home, down the busy main street of singles—Second Avenue—past Adam's Apple and

Friday's and Maxwell's Plum to her street . . . as cool as Bogart.

Sure, she wore contact lenses. Why not? Sure, she couldn't see in the dark. Did they think she was a bloody cat?

The courtroom had become a second home. She knew where the best toilet booth was, where the phones were, and about what time the judge had to go the bathroom or eat.

They gathered and waited. "Seats!"

Then "Rise."

Then "Seats."

"This court. . ." and so on. And Susan sat again in the hot barnlike room with its drooping flags, unmoving people, and the questionable majesty of the law.

Warren took his familiar stance before her. She must have done something terribly wrong to deserve this kind of torture.

"My last question to you was, 'Miss Landress, do you wear contact lenses?' I repeat the question hoping that the intervening hours have permitted you to acquire your normal calm and rest."

"Objection!" Fred said he didn't like the editorials. "Obviously, the defense attorney is trying to unsettle the complainant."

"Just answer the question," said the bored judge and mediator.

"I wear them once in a while; or glasses."

"Were you wearing either on the day in question?"

"I don't remember exactly."

"Wouldn't it make a difference in the way things appeared to you?"

"I suppose so."

191

"Then tell me, were you wearing them all the time that day?"

"I said, 'I don't remember exactly.'"

Warren seemed exasperated. He turned and shrugged at the jury, trying to evoke their sympathy over her stubbornness.

"Tell me, don't you take your contacts out in the evening, to rest your eyes?"

"Yes."

"Didn't you have them out that evening, when you went for your little relaxing walk in the park?"

"I guess so. I don't know."

"You guess! Miss Landress, were you wearing them or not?"

"If you say so."

"Will you please instruct the witness..."

"Miss Landress, it is obvious that neither contact lenses nor glasses were in your possession that night. Why can't you simply say yes or no?"

"No."

"Therefore, you were not able to see as well that night without them as you might had you worn them?"

"No."

"I'm through with my cross-examination, sir," said Warren with obvious disgust.

Fred stood up. The judge felt the least bit sorry for him, having been cheated out of his confession and then the button and now it seemed his one witness wasn't going to make it in time.

"Your Honor, the prosecution rests!"

After lunch, and back in her seat, she heard Warren calling his first witness, her roommate.

"Please call Miss Treadwell!" the judge directed the clerk who bellowed out her name with no response. Susan told Michaels that Anne had left a note about a quick trip to Montreal.

"Is Anne Treadwell in this courtroom?" Warren now stood up and looked around for her, then asked the clerk to call her again. The name ricocheted around the silent room but no Anne Treadwell came forward. Warren knew very well that she wouldn't. It was evident now that her quick trip to Montreal had been made to avoid testifying.

"I then call Michael Rose to the stand!" said Warren, and the heavy-set figure of Susan's former boss slowly walked forward to take the oath and testify. After he was fully at ease Warren began to question him.

"Was Susan Landress anxious to pose for you?"

"Objection!" Fred was up.

The judge asked him his grounds.

"Irrelevant, Your Honor, I. . ."

"I will not sustain on those grounds, but as to form. Mr. Warren, you know how to question a witness."

He was very humble. "Yes, Your Honor, I apologize to the Court." He faced the judge, then turned to the witness. "Now, Mr. Rose, prior to her posing for these pornographic. . ."

"Objection!" protested Fred.

". . .let me rephrase that. Prior to posing for these photos in one of which there appears to be a hand reaching toward her breast, did you have any conversation with her in which she made a statement reflecting on her attitude about posing for these collector's items?"

"Your Honor!" repeated Fred.

"The witness will answer the question."

"Yes, Your Honor. We did have a discussion. Her and me."

"When was this discussion?" Warren gloated.

"Before the pictures were taken."

"Where was this discussion?"

"In my private office."

"Your private office?"

"Yes."

"Who was present with you two while you were discussing her posing for these pictures in the private office?"

"Just her . . . and me."

"And what did you say to her?"

"I said we had this suntan oil account. I said we needed some test shots to see whether the oil looked like oil on skin and would she mind posing to help out."

"May I ask you what you mean when you say 'to see whether the oil looked like oil'?"

"Sometimes commonplace things don't photograph the way they actually are. Chocolate, for example, looks like mud."

"So you mean that you asked her to pose with this oil on her skin to see whether it photographed as oil?"

"Yes."

"And what did she say?"

"She asked me whether I thought she had a good enough figure for that sort of thing."

"Had you advised her up to then that she might have to pose for your photographs?"

"She must have presumed it. Anyway, she said she would only wear a bikini when I told her she had a great figure. And she has." Mike Rose smiled.

"What were her words, as well as you can remember?"

"Easy. When I said, 'You'll pose in the nude,' which

is necessary you see, because sometimes oil on part of the body like the face seems like sweat while on. . ."

"Go on."

"While on a stomach or legs, it's obviously shiny and has been put there. So she said, 'I don't want to.' But she pulled on this little bikini which left nothing to the imagination, and that was just as good as being nude, you might say."

"And during the subsequent shooting, did you have to force her, or threaten her with her job?"

"No siree! She fell into it natural. She understood it. She dug it. She took it from the absolute concept, don't you see?"

"That is all. Your witness."

Fred approached the man cautiously. It was as if he posed an unusual type of person with whom he had never had contact. "Mr. Rose, when you say, 'She understood it. She took it from the absolute concept,' what do you mean?"

Rose looked at him strangely, rubbed his chin and sighed impatiently. "Why I mean she dug the whole idea. She was with it. She knew."

"She knew what?"

"That the agency needed some good sexy test shots and. . ."

"Thank you. Now, Mr. Rose, during this shooting or prior to it did you or Miss Landress have any alcoholic drinks?"

"No, sir. Not on working time."

"Did you infer in your description of this assignment that it was part of her job . . . that is, expected of her?"

"Look here, mister, there's nothing wrong in modeling. My first wife posed in the nude and there are about fifty girls in the agency who pose in the nude. Things are different today."

"Then you and the models and the entire field in which you work do not consider the fact a girl poses in the nude to be degrading or immoral?"

"At two hundred an hour?"

"Thank you, Mr. Rose." Fred sat down with a smile.

"One more question," Warren asked. "We have seen the shots you took of Susan Landress covered with oil. In one of them there is a man's hand. It is suggestive to me. Is it so to you?"

"Your Honor, defense counsel is leading the witness."

"Sustained."

"I'll rephrase the question. Mr. Rose, are these shots, which you call test shots, to be shown to the client?"

"Not all of them, to be honest."

"I know that you'll be honest. Which ones would not have been shown to your suntan oil client?"

"Why, the ones with my hands on her, naturally!"

He stepped down to the indrawn breath of his audience. He must have known he had done a great deal of damage to her case. Susan knew the kind. She had met them. They were the sort of men who say, "No broad teases me and gets away with it!"

"Again I ask is Miss Anne Treadwell in this courtroom?"

But Anne was still in Montreal. "Out of the country."

Warren looked about the room as if expecting the girl to be seen walking down the aisle toward the witness stand.

Then he shrugged helplessly and spoke to Guy Masters.

"Watch this. You're about to get your money's worth."

"Your Honor," he started, waving an arm around the room, "Miss Treadwell has been subpoenaed as a witness for the defense. She is the girl who rooms with Susan Landress. She has seen fit not to respond to the subpoena and is now in Montreal, Canada. I therefore ask that a warrant be issued for her arrest! That she be held in contempt of court and when arrested be given the maximum criminal penalties!"

Fifteen

"Rape in the female mind outranks all others as a recurring fantasy," said Dr. Benjamin Katz. "It is a pleasurable fantasy among women. The current sexual permissiveness . . . the no-bra look, absence of underclothes causing visibility of breasts and buttocks, all have contributed to the explosive rise in the number of rapes, creating the impulse, particularly where sex has been on the mind of the attacker who might also have been drinking heavily."

Patricia looked at the little doctor through a cloud of cigarette smoke. He was an earnest fellow all right, who talked as if he were already on camera.

Reaching out for scientific opinion on rape, she had gone to visit this professor at Cornell University, where Katz conducted a course in forensic medicine. He had welcomed her and his favorite subject.

Dr. Katz relit his pipe and scratched his bald spot which gleamed under the chandelier, as he said: "In Philadelphia thirty-four percent of the city's rapes were between close neighbors or acquaintances. Now how can a lawman approach rape between members of a family and strangers in the same legal context?

"I believe the crime of rape should be differentiated under the law by comparative degree, as homicide is defined," he continued "Degrees should be designated, such as provoked, spontaneous, or psychopathic. And penalties should be spelled out commensurate with each degree and the trauma inflicted on the victim."

Patricia nodded agreement. "You're right!" she said. "Susan Landress had never met Guy Masters before. It was sudden, aggressive, and violent and she was foolish to enter a dark secluded area at that time of night. It's a wonder she wasn't murdered. . ."

Katz broke in. "The sexual deviant act of rape-aggression committed by Masters, with sex as the motive, was explosive, involved the seizure of absolute and instant control over his victim, and could have involved blows which might have killed her. The use of force against her should legally be evidence enough that she was raped and put up the utmost resistance. Masters may have tried to speak with her first, suggest a date, or just start an idle conversation. He might have threatened her verbally or tried to intimidate her or used a weapon to gain his desire.

"In two-thirds of the reported cases in the study in Philadelphia the more aggressive, intimidating methods were used. Any rape out-of-doors, as in this case, would start with violence to prevent discovery. Just as there are differences in motivation in manslaughter and premeditated homicide, there might very well be legal differences between the planned rape in which a certain woman is pre-selected and that of a casual passerby who triggers aggression and desire. Laws might well define the differences, once the relationship factor has been established. It would seem a man who plans to rape a neighbor has been more calculating and deliberately malicious in his crime than a man who reacts to a sudden impulse."

"Masters's lawyer could bring out that the defendant had been drinking, had never met the girl, and that it was a case of temporary insanity just for the effect upon the jury if nothing else," Patricia said.

"You're right. Liquor is often considered a general excuse for sexual permissiveness. It implies the offender's judgment was impaired, that he did not contrive or choose the geography or location of his impulsive act, nor had he planned it. As to planned or nonplanned rapes, it is interesting that violent and spontaneous rapes actually occur between single men and women, while the majority of planned rapes are perpetrated by gangs or groups and more likely involve taking the victim to some pre-planned location."

He went on: "It is an uncontrolled action in many cases. In others, such as planned rape where a man has an object under surveillance and works out a rape plan or when a gang rape is organized by a leader, then, of course, you have motivations of another sort to consider."

"I don't see why lawmakers don't take motive into consideration when they put away a rapist," said Patricia. "If he suddenly attacks a stranger in a burst of madness, it should be treated as temporary insanity and an unpremeditated act. On the other hand, when it is the result of planning it should be dealt with differently. Premeditated attacks are always dissimilar from aggression triggered by some compelling urge of the moment."

"Rape lurks in every man's mind. He sees a girl who appeals instantly. He wants her. He watches someone undress on stage. He wants her. But he waits until he gets home and can hop into bed with his consenting wife or girl friend. He is under control. It's the man who has no outlet the law is most concerned with."

"Doctor, the other day a policeman was indicted for raping a fifteen-year-old girl. He happened to be married with three kids at home. Are you telling me he was a man with no outlet?"

"The fact he was a policeman intrigues you, doesn't it? If he wasn't and was just any other man, would you find the story as reprehensible, salacious? Well, let me suggest that every man is a potential rapist—or under certain circumstances will attack a girl. Did the report state whether this fifteen-year-old girl was mature for her age, had perhaps led him on? No one is quite as informed about rape as a cop."

Dr. Katz added, "After all, they see it on the streets every day. Maybe this girl was the neighborhood whore, or maybe the cop was getting a divorce. Just because the record says he has a wife and three children doesn't automatically make his sex life happy. These are the factors that should be explored in this case. And you owe it to your listeners, Miss Rankin, to raise such points. Maybe then we'll know more about how to treat rape."

"What I worry about isn't how to treat rape or the rapist at this point. I'm too involved in the life of one Susan Landress and what the judge and jury will do to it. I can relate to one woman—not all women, once I'm involved with that one. You see, I'm a false feminist. I'm too much the mother to care about other people's children."

He smiled, stood up, scratched his bald spot and said, "No, you're not. Take this one situation about which you are worried, and let it be the umbrella case for the female of the species. Continue to let Susan Landress tell her story through you to your listeners. They will surely identify better with the living example than with the statistics."

It was her dismissal. She walked to his class with him and returned to New York City.

Sixteen

"I make a motion to dismiss," said Warren opening his summation, "on the grounds of insufficient evidence; that in the absence of proper and preponderant evidence required to uphold a verdict of guilt, that reason and justice dictate that the defendant must be presumed innocent."

"I will reserve decision on that, pending what the jury finds," the judge responded. "Are you now ready with your closing arguments?"

Since he did not have the advantage of the last contact with the jurors before they marched into the back room to deliberate, Warren had put a great deal of thought to the arguments he would use. His summation would be short, eloquent, and rational. He had spent the evening indulging his taste for vin rosé, veal with wine sauce, and a dash of absinthe over his final cup of lemon sherbet. Then he had gone off into his usual deep sleep without a worry. Now his client sat next to him, orderly, composed. He rose to his six feet, moved out from his table, adjusted the black suit over his thin body, and spoke.

"Ladies and gentlemen of the jury. . ." he began. "Honorable Court, you have now heard all the evidence with your own ears. Nothing I say here now should be interpreted to make any difference in the facts as you heard them, for neither I nor the prosecution can tell you anything more about the evidence in this case. You have heard the evidence through the direct testimony of the witnesses, and you will see the evidence in the form of exhibits on file with this court. The evidence is all there for you. In my mind the facts are clear that there should be no doubt as to the innocence of Guy Masters."

Warren moved away from the jury, went back to his table, picked up a few papers, and dropped them.

"Let us review this so-called evidence together. We heard the policeman who states that he observed Guy Masters trying to open a door. Now the criminal law has not yet progressed to the point where it's a crime to open a door. And I want you to recall there were no burglary tools, or anything of that kind, found on him. After this fine member of the New York City police force completed his testimony, we heard another sterling character, a licensed physician who doesn't take notes and examines two thousand women a year but remembers this particular woman more than the others. In other words, out of two thousand rapes a year—two thousand gynecological examinations—this particular woman, whom he saw for approximately thirty minutes, he remembers with perfect clarity. From this brief encounter, with no written notes, he recalls the case. As a physician he professionally is required to record his observations. Therefore, this man's testimony should be totally disregarded.

"The next character in this charade was the complainant herself. And we got some very definite testimony." He added with a hushed voice, as if deeply concerned over it, "Evidence to the effect that the light level was such that she couldn't even see who attacked her—if, in fact, she was attacked. We know she's living with a lesbian. That she left her lawful husband on their wedding night, mind you, and I think from this we can infer a great desire to do injury to men because there is a genuine hatred here of the male sex in this particular woman."

He paused, looked around the room, and then said, "She is not an innocent little girl, despoiled. She revels in her sexuality. You saw the pictures. She enjoys looking sexy, arousing the sexual interest of men. You saw the pictures! His hands on her body. The testimony of this particular witness is so unreliable—so clouded in mystery, so unfounded, and so biased that you cannot convict an innocent man—a working man—on such information.

"This woman is literally 'living in sin' every day of her life posing for photographs that if, in fact," he whispered in horror, "they were ever viewed by younger persons. . ." his voice showed his deep concern—"might excite them to—act—strangely," he finished, his voice a deep whisper. Then after straightening his shoulders, as if to face an unhappy but inevitable fact, "We are all familiar with pornography in this country. It is running rampant; undermining religious and social restraints, the backbone of decent family life. It has led youth to believe in promiscuity, in sexual deviations, and in inhuman acts of sex, one upon another. Sitting in this court today we have the very perpetrator of such lewd and disgusting pornographic photographs . . . a woman who thinks absolutely nothing of revealing herself before a camera for all the world to see with a male hand pawing her disgustingly!"

What he had just said obviously affected Warren very much, for he took out a huge white handkerchief and wiped his face thoroughly. Recovering himself, he went on, "So that's the cast of characters for the prosecution! An immoral woman, a police officer who saw a man trying to find a bathroom, and a physician who forgot to write down his findings on the case but remembers them. I would say to you, ladies and gentlemen of the jury, if you were to return a conviction in this case I would lose my faith in the jury system. It would be absolutely incredible that a man could be deprived of his freedom by such hogwash. Now this is what we call a 'rape case.'"

Warren stopped pacing and stood nearer the judge as if by proximity he could acquire judicial status. "Whether we like the name or not, rape is a terrible crime. Nobody is going to deny that. But if a rape has been committed," he sighed, "it should be very clear in your minds that Guy Masters had nothing whatsoever to do with that rape. And this Court will instruct you—and I urge you to listen carefully to the instruction—that in the prosecution of a so-called rape case the prosecutor must bring out certain substantiating evidence because we don't send people to prison here—as in Russia—on suspicion, or because we don't like their face, or their creed, or their color. This is a land of justice," he intoned with dignity. "Thank God for it!" Warren assumed the appearance of a founding father as he added that touch, thinking to himself that mother, God, and country rarely failed.

"Now the prosecution is going to have to prove to you that there was forcible penetration." He paused, looking at some of the women jurors. "Now, I'm sorry if I embarrass you. One of the questions is whether Susan Landress was penetrated against her will. And I submit to you that there is not a shred of reliable testimony on that fact except the words coming to you through the mouth of Susan Landress, who couldn't even see what was going on.

"She couldn't have seen the person to the right or left of her in that same light, even wearing glasses! And I say to you that this prosecution has not proved force through any means except the good doctor, who just happens to remember this woman out of four thousand similar cases! I submit to you that there is nothing to connect the complainant's bruises with Guy Masters, much less with a rape! I say that these wounds could have been selfinflicted.

"Have you heard anything here today which, in your mind, would possibly prove Guy Masters committed any kind of criminal act? He didn't live with anybody in a relationship of sodomy! He's not a thief! He has no criminal record! Susan Landress has a criminal record. This is the type of person that we're dealing with." He became almost sad as he asked, "And this is the woman who wants to send a man away for twenty-five years?"

Almost indignant, he said, "Ladies and gentlemen of the jury, you've heard the testimony of Officer Melo that he saw Guy Masters trying to find a bathroom." Warren shouted it out with indignation, as if the entire police force had tried to stop the natural functions of the human body.

He looked at each of them as if awaiting an answer. "The law states I don't have to put Guy Masters on the stand and that you're not to draw any inference from my decision not to. You have heard the complainant's former employer tell you that she was absolutely delighted in posing for those photographs.

Take a good long look at those photographs. Take a look.

"And this is the woman who asks you to believe her every word? Ladies and gentlemen of the jury, there should be no doubt in your mind as to what you must do. I am asking you to listen to the charges of the judge and make your decision in accordance with what you've heard here, with the facts, not with what I have told you. I could only highlight the total unreliability of every single witness who came before you. I ask you to listen to the Court carefully and if there is the slightest doubt of his guilt in your mind, you know you must find for the defendant, Guy Masters. Thank you."

"Your summation is all you have. Keep talking and make your points. You don't have many but you know what they are." D. P. Scott was retiring. He was almost bored with the matter of *The People* v. *Masters*. It had started out so well, but that old bastard Warren had won.

Fred walked into the courtroom with a straight back and wearing a blue suit. He looked around briefly, saw Patricia seated in the rear, and hoped to God he wouldn't disgrace himself or prove incapable in front of her.

"I want to be there. That's all there is to it," she had said that morning over the phone. "And I'm going. You can't stop me."

"Well, no taping and no pictures. I'm going to give it a good school try!"

Now, before the assemblage, he began.

"Honorable Court, honorable adversary, ladies and gentlemen of the jury, and spectators." He seemed small in contrast to the man they had just listened to, but he made up for it in vigor, turning quickly from the court to his adversary and to the people assembled. "As worthy counsel has stated, you've heard all the evidence in this case. And he has explained it to you as he sees it.

"What controls this case, however, is what you've heard from the mouths of the witnesses. The first thing we should get straight is who is on trial here. Guy Masters is on trial, not Susan Landress. She had a humiliating and brutal act committed against her. It was not one of those things you can pass off lightly as a joke. This is an innocent, virtuous woman, just like any of your wives, or sisters, or mothers. She was strolling lawfully in a city park when viciously attacked, her clothes ripped off against her will, then forced down to the cold ground, and violently attacked. A man sexually abused her against her will. He then attacked her again, compelling her to submit to a sexually deviate assault. And then he left her there, abandoned like a sick and wounded animal which had served his purpose.

"This was a vicious sexual surprise-attack. The man who looks so demure, and so cool about this whole thing, didn't even take the stand. . ."

Warren stood up immediately. "Objection! That fact cannot be used against him, Your Honor!"

The judge sustained and instructed the jury to completely disregard the remark, "Which should not have been made and which counsel knew should not have been made!" He frowned at Michaels who took a fresh stance.

"May I continue, Your Honor?" asked Michaels.

"Proceed," the judge responded.

"As I was saying, you have heard witnesses testify that this woman was raped . . . and the evidence

209

shows she was raped very much against her will . . . that she struggled as much as was humanly possible. You've heard the police, you've heard the doctor who examined her, and you've heard the complainant Susan Landress, in tears, tell you in detail what happened to her. Now at this point there shouldn't be any doubt as to what you have to do . . . must do, if you care for your wives, your children, or your family. If you don't care. . ." his voice rose, "and if you think all this is some kind of joke, then go ahead, let Guy Masters walk the street. Let him rape someone else, now that he's gotten away with this one. Maybe you'll be next!" He pointed at two elderly school teachers who recoiled visibly at the thought. "And see how you feel about it then. If you jurors want to condone rape as being no more serious than going through a red light and treat it as commonplace, if you think American men should go around jumping upon American women day or night, picking out whom they wish, no matter whether she is young or old, your wife or your mother, pulling her into shadows, tearing off her clothes, treating her like a willing slave to their desires, sexually abusing her while she (perhaps it is your wife) screams in vain and curses the day you let this man go free . . . then, find this man innocent! I'm telling you, if you don't care, that's what you will do!

"Now, let me ask you what have you actually heard in his defense. We've heard nothing but a fabrication. Sure this lady posed once for some pictures while nearly nude. My goodness, she comes from a community—a beach community—where everyone goes around in the briefest of swim suits. They live in the almost-nude on the beach. It doesn't mean the same for girls to be nearly nude as it does in New York City. And you heard her boss confess that the agency they use for models has a goodly supply of girls who regularly pose in the nude. In magazines such as *Vogue* and *Harper's Bazaar* there are perfectly decent photographs of women in lingerie, isn't that so?" He looked directly at a young female juror who instinctively nodded back. "And besides, Susan Landress is aware of this. She didn't make any deep secret of it, as if she had been luring the man on. Does that make her a ready, willing victim for this man's attack or any man's attack against her will?

"Let me put it another way. Let us presume that one of you on the jury committed an income tax fraud. Let's say you wrote something off to charity which you never actually gave. Does that mean that a strange man in a park has the right to rip off your clothes, pin you down on the cold ground, and rape you! Does that mean a man can leap on you—and abuse you?

"You have been told about a criminal record. What is this horrible criminal record? She was shoplifting! What kind of crime is this? It's a crime of temptation. We're not dealing with a wealthy person here. She had to earn a living and care for her invalid mother while her brother fought in Viet Nam. Now I'm not condoning what she was forced to do to get something to wear, but I am saying that is no reason why someone, someone who has been convicted and paid her debt to society, should be automatically abused by anyone else ... that she is automatically elected for rape in the streets.

"The defense has even stooped to accusing Susan Landress of being a lesbian. Why? He had no evidence, nothing tangible which he could legally submit to you. He simply wanted to turn you against her. To prejudice you. Even if we had gone so far as to admit Susan Landress was a lesbian, that would still give us no reason to countenance an attack of violence—a crime against her person. What you heard about her wasn't evidence! Guy Masters is charged with rape. Rape One. What has her alleged past relationship with someone else to do with that? It is meant to mislead you ... to influence you against her. But she isn't on trial! It's like saying Hitler slew six million Jews, but that was all right; one of them was a very bad man!" He paused to let it sink in.

"May I ask you, ladies and gentlemen, would you want your neighbor to defend your character? How many of you in New York would ask your neighbor to speak about your private life, to testify to your behavior? How many of you indeed even know your neighbor!"

Fred walked over to the bench, stood looking up at the judge as if to measure him and then turned swiftly to the jury. "Ladies and gentlemen, I would like to do something now about the lights—with the Court's permission. I ask that the lights be turned off in this courtroom!"

No one spoke. Then the entire room looked at the judge. He looked at Fred, then at the clerk, and said, "This court is in recess for twenty minutes. Mr. Michaels, will you meet me in my chambers?"

There, seated before a glass of water, he asked Fred, "What in the name of God are you asking me to turn the lights off for? You can't be serious!"

"I am. I know that you can deny my request. But go along with me. There is one switch. I have investigated. Get a guard to throw that switch and the People may have a chance against Masters."

"I'm not here to take sides. I'll throw the switch. But, young man, you'd better have something tangible. I've got a future that is worth more than yours."

"Why?"

"There's so little left of it."

When the room had filled again, Fred stood up and requested the lights be turned off again "at my signal." The judge nodded. Warren started to get up. The judge stared him down.

Fred said, "Ladies and gentlemen of the jury, please focus your eyes on a distant object across the room—something or someone. Now . . . . . . switch!" He raised his hand. The room was in absolute darkness. "Now look around you. Do you see anything? Of course you don't see anything because your eyes aren't yet accustomed to the sudden darkness, just as if you had walked into a dark park from the brightly lighted street. Now, if I may, I ask you to wait in this darkness for three minutes. I won't address you for those three minutes. I just want you to get accustomed to the absence of light just as someone out at night like Susan Landress and Guy Masters got accustomed to the darkness."

No one moved. Someone coughed. The judge drank some water.

"Now!" said Fred in the darkened room. "It's three minutes. I haven't turned on any lights. Look around you. You can begin to see everything now, can't you? Because your eyes have become used to the light conditions. This is the trick the defense would play on you! If you go into a dark movie theatre from the bright sunlight, you don't see anything at first because your eyes have not become accustomed to the darkness. But within minutes your eyes adjust and you are able to see about you, even some detail.

"It is quite obvious," he said in measured tones, "that Susan Landress could see Guy Masters very well! Well enough to identify him. When she saw Masters, he was right on top of her, only inches away."

He waited one moment and then ordered, "Switch on!"

The room was a blaze of light and the jurors began rubbing their eyes and looking about.

Glancing from one juror to the other as if addressing each individually, he continued, "I appeal to your sense of impartiality. Let us assume all the things the victim has been accused of are true—admit all these things—does that make her fair game for a vicious rape attack? We must get this man and all men like him off our streets—off your streets. There is no other way to do this than to show lustful, evil men with a desire to harm, to commit crimes against persons such as this, that our city will not stand for it. The women of this city will not condone it —nor with God's help and yours will the law!"

The jury looked back at him with an undeniable calm, as if what he was saying might be exceedingly important to him—but to them. . .?

"Look at this man!" He swung his finger at Masters. "There he sits—the rapist! Will you let him do this to your sister? To your beloved wife? No! A thousand times no! He must be kept off the streets so that he can't continue his despicable crimes. This man must be put away."

Suddenly Fred knew what was going on. The entire jury stared back, impassive. They were just unimpressed, waiting for it to be over so they could go in the room there—take a quick vote for acquittal, and get out and go home.

The only one who didn't seem to know he was going to go free was Guy Masters. He leaned toward his lawyer. "For God's sake, he's got me hung!" Warren motioned him to silence. "Later!" he whispered, with a benevolent look.

Fred seemed to run out of breath—but he went on, almost with desperation. "I plead with you. I urge you as peace-loving, clean-minded, law-abiding citizens, rid our streets of men of this kind, men like Guy Masters, who is guilty of first degree rape. Put him away, ladies and gentlemen, where he cannot rape another girl like this one ever again!" He sat down.

D.P. put his arm on Fred's shoulder and squeezed.

"Did I make an impression?" the young DA inquired anxiously.

"No, I don't think so. But you tried hard and you'll understand the vagaries of rape cases from now on."

Warren and Masters walked behind the throng which ambled its way out and up the aisle. They passed Susan, Michaels, and Scott. "You wait until they go out. While they're out, you die. Then you pray that by some idiotic fluke they don't find you guilty." Masters was silent, fear building up in him.

Susan tried to smile. "It made me feel better listening to you. Somebody understands, that's all I could keep thinking. Thanks," she said, "thanks again—for everything."

He looked at her and smiled. This woman had guts. Maybe she had been a bit naive when she first came to New York. Maybe the last few months had made her streetwise, as the cops called it. But the humiliating experience and abrasive treatment had wounded her deeply. He took her hand.

"All we can do is leave it to the jury. Now the judge charges them." Out of the corner of his eye he saw Patricia brooding, looking directly at him.

When they returned, he looked at Susan who stared up at Judge Rosenman. He sat in his seat looking like a wise old owl. After a pause the judge began:

"It now becomes the Court's duty to charge the jury. This means that the Court instructs you as to the law governing this case. You are to accept that law, and that law alone, and apply it to the facts of the case."

While he droned on, Susan wondered if she, too, could accept the law and that law alone if he let Masters go free, if he so charged the men and women up there. Wasn't there some other law which said "An eye for an eye," which was a higher law? The words came to mind, "Man's extremity is God's opportunity," and they comforted her. What had they to do with her situation now? She listened to what the judge was saying up there. He was now talking about witnesses.

"The law says you should consider the conduct of the witnesses and their demeanor. How did the witnesses impress you? Was there any attempt to stretch the truth? Was there any evidence of bias?

"The Court of Appeals has said in this state that every trial should be a search for the truth. Your duty is to search for the truth and—having found it to your satisfaction—to report your findings to the Court by means of a proper verdict under the law as the Court lays it down."

As he went on, she listened with half an ear until he came to a part which involved Masters not taking the stand. He seemed actually to be excusing him!

"In every criminal case, I repeat, in a criminal case there is the rule which states that no defendant is compelled to take the witness stand. By his plea of 'not guilty' you see he has already denied the charges against him and it puts the burden of responsibility upon the prosecution to prove guilt beyond a reasonable doubt.

"The defense has produced proof that the com-

216

plainant, Susan Landress, had previously been convicted of shoplifting. Now, you may not permit this fact to influence your verdict or determination in this case. If a situation in this case existed in which her veracity was an issue and she had been proved guilty of perjury, then her capacity to tell the truth might have bearing and you might have to apply that fact to this case. This is a matter of credibility. And on that point the law is very clear.

"I must also caution you as to witnesses who are brought on, who themselves may be tarred with the brush of immorality. Now, you must ignore this and rely only on your own sound, reasoned judgment and exclude dislike or prejudice; the morals of others are not to concern you. You must only consider the testimony of that witness and not discard it merely because the witness is of tainted character or has himself or herself engaged in debauchery."

Ah! That would include her boss. Debauchery indeed!

"As to rape: you must determine whether vaginal penetration was committed without the consent of the alleged victim. This is defined as 'physical force that overcomes earnest resistance that places a person in fear of immediate death or serious physical injury.'

"Now I will define 'earnest resistance.' It means using all of her powers of resistance and defense, and all her powers to summon others to her aid. It is also true and you must consider this: that if, notwithstanding the use of force, she finally consents to the sexual act and her will ceases to defend against the consummation, then there is no crime.

"Rape is the word you must consider. For the defendant, Guy Masters, stands here indicted for the crime of rape. Before you can get down to your individual and collective decision of whether he is or is not guilty of rape you must first find that he did indeed engage in sexual intercourse with the female named. In this context the definition states 'Sexual intercourse occurs upon penetration, however slight, in any orifice.' Thus the word and act of penetration alone marks the boundary between rape and, let's say, 'molestation,' sexual contact, love-play, or other sexual intimacies. Penetration must be into the vagina, otherwise it is considered deviate sexual intercourse or sodomy, not rape. It must be more than sexual contact. There must be penetration, to be an act of rape, that is. Now there need be no physical satisfaction. It is not necessary that the man be satisfied or attain completion by orgasm. And emission is not required to constitute sexual intercourse under the law."

Susan's mind wasn't on what he said. Her thoughts had returned to the night of her attack. Perhaps his definitions had caused it, but she very clearly relived the moment when Masters, brutal and sweating and cursing, had attacked her. She almost screamed but caught herself with hand over mouth to hear the judge smilingly refer to rape as not unlike burglary in one respect.

"There is an analogy between the two. One proceeds far enough to justify a charge of burglary when one has entered into a structure and passed the line of portal, even if one goes no further. So one is guilty of sexual penetration and rape without regard to one's failure to appease one's lust. Now, it must be found that the defendant engaged in sexual intercourse with the complainant, a woman not married to him, and that this was affected by forcible compulsion. In other words, sexual intercourse must be affected by *force* to be rape. This disclosure may be dependent solely upon the veracity of the complainant and be unsupported by other evidence. In that case it is not sufficient evidence. Identification must connect the defendant with the rape and the perpetration of rape. There has to be proof of force and there has to be proof of lack of consent.

"You have been informed of the requisite elements of the crime of rape. You have been instructed that if any one of the elements is lacking as you perceive and analyze the probative value of the evidence, you cannot convict of rape and you should examine the evidence further to determine if any lesser crime developed by that evidence has been proven. If, however, all elements of rape have been present, and beyond a reasonable doubt have been proven, then you must render a verdict of guilty. As you deliberate remember that your decision must be unanimous if your verdict is to stand."

Masters was nervous. He couldn't wait to lean over and whisper to Warren.

"Did we win?"

"Shut up and walk quietly out of here," he was told.

They waited in the empty corridor outside the now-deserted courtroom. No more argument. No more persuasion. It was in the hands of the jury. Masters walked to the fountain, doused his cigarette, and took a sip of water. "How long?"

Warren watched him, smiled, shrugged his shoulders.

"Come on," said Masters. "I'll buy you a cup of coffee." He started toward the stairway. Warren stood firm. "When it's open and shut either way— guilty or not guilty—they come back fast."

Warren unfolded his paper, started to read the drama page.

"Hey! Aren't you worried?"

219

"Sure. About the weather. Your case is predictable."

"What'll it be? Please tell me."

"Did you do it?" asked Warren.

Masters looked for a cigarette, searched his pocket for a match, pretended not to hear. "Gotta light?" he asked.

"Did you?"

"Pretty soon we'll know, won't we?"

What was he answering? "Sure, pretty soon they'll come in with their verdict. It's either yes or no. So tell me now. You did, didn't you?"

"Why? So you can say you got a man off who really had raped the girl? Is that it?"

"Only one percent of the rapists get time. Mostly they get off."

"Like I will. You heard the testimony. What would you say?"

"I'd say you raped a girl but she couldn't prove it."

"What's that man at the door waving at?"

"It's us. They must have come back. Let's see what the jury found."

It was the clerk.

"It's off until tomorrow. The judge has called for the court to reconvene in the morning."

"Jesus, I'll have to wait until tomorrow. I can't stand it."

"This may be your last day of freedom," Warren said grimly.

Seventeen

Susan didn't remember getting home.

She did remember starting to pack her bags. There were some things at the cleaner's around the corner and some laundry the washing machine wouldn't take; so she started out the door. When she reached the street she realized that for some reason it was dark. She looked at her wrist watch. It was eight! She had lost three hours somewhere!

She turned around and started home. For a long while she walked up York Avenue and then it came to her that she had passed her street and was five blocks north. She saw a cab and hailed it, giving the young man her address.

He turned in surprise, looked at her carefully.

"Are you sure?"

"Of what? What did you say?"

He shrugged. "It's so few blocks," he replied. He took her to her door. She fumbled for the key—couldn't find it. Tried the handle and walked in. She had left it open? What was happening to her?

She realized her mind was pulling blanks. She walked over to the telephone and picked it up. There was no dial tone. She waited a moment, thought she heard someone on the other end and said, "Hello?"

"Hello? Is that you?"

"Who is this?" She thought she recognized the voice, but it couldn't be her brother. They must have dialed simultaneously.

"It's Dougie. What in the hell is going on there, Sis?"

"What do you mean?"

"I just got the *Evening Outlook*. It says you were raped. Honey ... it's me ... your brother ... Why didn't you. . ."

Then he started to cry. Dougie, the war vet from Nam, the holder of citations for valor, began to cry. Then there was a crackling and she was cut off. Jesus, was she dreaming . . . had he really called her? She hung up, waited a moment, then dialed her home in California. The line was busy. She hung up again and turned to the empty luggage facing her . . . and the dirty clothes stuffed into a pillow case.

She would leave. The phone rang again. It was her brother.

He had control of himself now. He tried to speak.

"Tell me . . . what happened?"

"It's all true. I should have stayed home."

"Mother ... it's Mother. The shock was very ... very bad on her. People began calling. You know how she is. She denied it at first . . . then it sank in; there must be some truth. Then the TV. It's on TV, Susan. Out here."

"It's on TV, here, Dougie . . . it's on everywhere!"

"Should I come . . . I mean do you need me now?"

222

"Oh, no. Don't come. I'm getting out. I'm leaving. Now. I'm leaving here, Dougie."

"Susan . . . Sue?"

"Yes?" Her voice was a whisper. A small child asking for help.

"Don't come home now. Why don't I meet you in . . . meet me in L.A. and we'll find a place for you . . . until Mother. . ."

"Never mind. It's alright. I won't embarrass Mother . . . never mind . . . never mind anyone!"

She hung up and when he called her back again she just stared at the telephone while it rang. One-two-three-four-five-six-seven-eight-nine-ten . . . then it stopped.

No one. She had no one. She would call Fred as a token courtesy. She dialed his home telephone.

Fred couldn't have been more depressed. Everything was going wrong.

They had shot the whole thing down—all the way—and all he could do was pick up the pieces. Every man for himself.

"You talked a lot, and you repeated yourself," D. P. Scott had said, "but it's a common failing in a new assistant DA. You'll learn a lot if you listen to the legal aids. They get more practical cases in a year than you or a member of a criminal law firm will get in ten years. And they know the ropes. You should have gotten a second confession—in the jail—under your own supervision. You should have had Mrs. McElroy under standing subpoena. Why did you permit her to leave the country?"

How could you answer questions after the fact? Fred took Patricia to Le Cafe des Artistes and let

Charles order them something to eat. The gang from the TV station and the network guys were there. At the bar. Fred and Patricia sat in the dining room holding hands in silence, trying to forget that the jury would reconvene in the morning to decide his future.

"Why your future?"

"No one blames me if another rapist gets off?"

"I'll be down there with a crew tomorrow morning. Whatever happens, my newsman will protect your image. What else can a woman do?"

"Nothing," he said. "You've done everything a woman could do."

After the poached bass with hollandaise they went to his apartment. The telephone was ringing steadily. She handed it to him. "Susan, for you?"

"What in the name of God is she calling me for at this hour?"

"I'm splitting. I've had enough!" Susan was saying. "I don't guess you'll need me tomorrow when the jury comes in."

"Of course I'll need you. You can't go now."

"What for? I feel sick. I'm leaving right now."

"It's a matter of ethics. You've stood up and called a man a rapist. The jury may come back with further questions and the judge may need you to amplify a point. It's just wisest to be there. My God, Susan, after all this!"

She didn't answer. Then, "What time do you want me?"

"Ten o'clock. I'll pick you up. I'll drive you down. I'll be there at nine-thirty. Now don't disappear. Don't fail me. You are needed."

She hung up. "Needed!" That was a funny word.

Patricia slowly read her speech into the tape recorder for use when her voiceover would accompany the TV camera shot of Susan Landress coming up the steps of the Criminal Courts building.

"The New York Police Department has just released the latest figures on crimes against persons in this city. At this moment, also, the FBI has issued its quarterly statement on rape in this nation. During the last eight months, forcible rape has increased by 40.5 percent over the same period last year. It is a national disgrace—a national disaster for women.

"This is a woman's war. And we are going to ask men to enlist in the fight with us—against their own archaic chauvinist attitudes—now!

"As a man who has handled one rape case from beginning to end, Mr. Frederick Michaels, Assistant District Attorney for the City of New York, has come up with a solution which we hope will be brought before our lawmakers. It would make rape a civil as well as a criminal action in which a convicted rapist becomes subject to imprisonment and heavy fines. His proposal also provides that bail be increased to thirty thousand dollars when there is sufficient evidence, such evidence to be determined by the court.

"This will do two things: it will slow down a rapist who is sick and who is out for psychopathic thrills, and it will keep him in jail until his trial. Rapists repeat their crime. It will also permit rape victims some hope of recompense for the ordeal of testifying —as Susan Landress has done."

Patricia sat in Fred's Porsche. After the foreman had notified the clerk that the jury had reached a decision, she intended to race up to the fourth floor and be ready in court. Below, her men would be stationed to catch the departing principles.

"Get Susan Landress. Get a close-up! I don't care if she holds her handbag to her face or is crying openly. I want it!" Those were orders from the producer, and Joe Fontana meant it. "I've had it with the sob-sister approach to this case. I can't wait until Patricia is off that subject and gets back to hard news!"

The cameraman blinked. "Jesus, Joe. This *is* news!"

Joe Fontana looked at the crowd which had already begun to gather and to find seats inside. "Okay, Robert old boy. Just do as I say and get that girl coming out. Don't go all soft and gooey over her. She asked for it."

Patricia read over her commentary, tucked it into her purse after making the tape, and sought words for her ad lib.

Fred had taken his seat with Susan. Across the aisle, Warren whispered to his client, "Just because your case hit the papers through some fluke—probably because I am handling it—I don't want you to get the idea you are some kind of celebrity. You have been charged with a crime I think you probably committed—a crime calling for twenty-five years imprisonment. And if this jury—which I have played on like Paderewski at his piano—comes in with a 'Not guilty,' I don't want to see a jerk, a smile, or a grin. Not a word or a move. Freeze! Do you hear? The press is back there and over there and up there near the bench, and they will have men and women looking at your face and artists sketching you, and if you *blink*, they'll catch it. I don't want a sigh of relief and don't you walk over to thank the jurors. Don't even move. Is that perfectly clear?"

"Yeah," Masters shrugged. He felt free. That's all that mattered. Soon, he'd get the fuck out of here and go up to Boston. His mother owned a big restaurant there. He could work and be with her. Just get him away!

"Are you listening? You look far away,"

"I'm in Boston slingin' hash and counting money. My mom's got a new place. She wants me. I'll go there. I'll blow this town."

"I don't care if you disappear off the face of the earth. But right now there are two alternatives. One is 'Not guilty' and I've instructed you in that. When they say it, if they do, stay in your seat. I will take your arm and you and I will walk out of court. I may be congratulated, but not you. This will have been a matter of masterly legal maneuver, not your innocence, and lawyers know that. And if they come out and say, 'Guilty as charged,' or with any minor variation of that, I want you to sit down and stay down. You will have to stand when the foreman has handed his decision in writing to the clerk and the clerk passes it to the judge. You will stand straight—head forward with no frown or grin. Then when they say, 'Guilty!' you are not to faint, pretend to faint, or scream, or cry out."

"What do you mean, 'when they say, "Guilty"?' I thought I would be free."

Warren took his shoulder in his long fingers and squeezed. Masters looked at him. "I don't know what they'll say, so you don't. I'm preparing you for either. Now sit still and be quiet and say your prayers."

When would she get out? Fred had picked her up at nine-thirty. Her bag was in her car. She would get a ticket for Chicago. A bus was leaving at two. She had the money ready in her purse. She felt for it. It was

227

there. She withdrew her hand and rubbed her fingers together. Where had the time gone? It was ten-thirty and she couldn't remember the drive down to court. Or how she happened to have a coffee stain on her blouse. Had they stopped for coffee? The room was hot and getting hotter. It was hot for October. Yes, very hot.

She felt, rather than heard, what was going on in the room. Over there two men sat in a huddle as people were crowding into the room. They seemed disturbed by the clamor. A large fat woman sat down behind her and began to blow her nose. She rattled the *Daily News* and blew again. Up front the clerk was standing and suddenly stood straighter. "All rise." He kept saying, "All rise!"

Then Judge Rosenman came in, his robes swirling like skirts, and he sat carefully down while she and everyone else remained standing.

He would send Masters away for twenty-five years. You could tell from his face how kindly he was. A slow crooked smile came over her face. Susan didn't feel young anymore. "Yes," she said aloud, loud enough for Fred to hear her, "that man will send Masters to jail for twenty-five years for what he did to me."

The jury filed in and slowly took seats. The judge turned to the foreman. "Have you reached a verdict?" There was complete silence from the five hundred spectators.

The foreman, a large man with a serious red face, said, "We have, Your Honor." No one moved. The judge asked, "Please read the verdict."

"We, the jury, find the defendant, Guy Masters, not guilty."

He sat down.

There was no rush to leave. People came out in groups, talking, nudging, as one or another recognized a participant and pointed him out. "There's D. P. Scott, with Fred Michaels; Scott's the top lawyer in the DA's Rape Squad." Or, "That's the cop who brought him in." They seemed to be waiting for someone. Was it Susan or Masters?

Patricia couldn't tell. Her men had taken the build-up shot and now were waiting. One man was stationed at the door to get the key figures as they came through. "The guy to get is Warren." He had surely screwed up the young DA.

"How about the victim?"

"Fontana wants her, one way or another. Get her!"

Patricia recalled later they had called her "the victim." Men knew after all. It had been a smart old fox, a hard-boiled war horse, against a kid. She knew what Fred would do. He had told her that last night on the island. "If I lose this case, I'll start working on rape laws with even greater fervor. I'll. . ."

"You'll take the next case, maybe fraud, and worry about that. I know you, Fred."

"Yeah, just a worrier. But I could use someone like you to help me do it. Does that appeal?"

Her reaction had been his answer.

Now that this case was over, they still had one another. But what about Susan?

What was she doing? Sitting all alone in this big empty hall. Everyone but a few stragglers had gone. She must go. But where? The people sitting next to her had mumbled something about, "Tough luck. See you around."

See her? Where? Why?

She stood up, placed her heavy leather purse over her shoulder and started out.

Outside in the hallway, people were jamming into

the room she had just left. A voice was complaining, "These fuckin' prostitutes clutter up our courts. We oughta just let 'em go." The lady cop walked past her, her arm on a tall thin black girl.

Susan's mind was far away . . . on the beach and a wave was slowly breaking . . . huge and heavy and it was going to hit her. She had started off, away from the court and the city and all those people—and found herself looking for a ladies room and then she just walked past it. The wave was engulfing her now.

"Surf's up!" Dougie called as he ran past her. He had his board with him. The sun was very hot on her pink shoulders. Mom was up there on the cliff watching. The wave came down, its edges curling first, then it seemed to tumble completely—all the way, a hundred yards to either side and for some strange reason Dougie was under it and the board under him flew up and came crashing down—and she saw blood.

Out in the street the sun was hot. It was noon and the lunch hour crush rushed, elbowed, bumped into her, tossing her about aimlessly. She moved into the crowd—under the wave of people—and disappeared.